HORSES FO⟶ ___

Nicky,
Congratulations on an
excellent ECC. Conference.

Islay.   (May 2022)

We hope you enjoy reading this
as much as we have enjoyed writing it

HORSES FOR LIFE

Dream Big — Aim High — One Life to Live

by

Pammy Hutton FBHS and Islay Auty FBHS

YOUCAXTON PUBLICATIONS
OXFORD & SHREWSBURY

ISBN 978-1-913425-53-1
Published by YouCaxton Publications 2020
YCBN: 01

YouCaxton Publications
www.youcaxton.co.uk

Preface

HRH The Princess Royal

BUCKINGHAM PALACE

This book is an important read for anyone, at any stage in their life, wishing to understand horses. The role that the horse can play in the lives of so many people, whether able bodied, with a range of disabilities or other disadvantages is highlighted, and clearly explains the horse's value and future in Society. Some of the chapters give us an insight to some of the values in life worth preserving. There are some refreshing views and lessons learnt from being open minded and practical.

The authors' lives have run along almost parallel lines during their early years, unbeknown to them as they started to write this book. Their love of horses shines through and some useful tips from them and their top class riders, trainers and professionals, who have contributed are helpful to those with experience or even those not connected to horses. Issues are covered in and out of the horse world from the authors' practical experiences of life. Like people, no two horses are the same. This book helps us to broaden our outlooks, never forget what went before and to respect our horses and their abilities as much as each others.

Anne

This book is dedicated to Nancy Nash, dear friend of Islay and Pammy. Nancy was a special lady, rider, owner.(daughter of Lorna Johnstone – Olympic rider see Chapter 3) Pammy and and Islay incidentally rode Nancy's mare 'Gretel' (Excelssissima) up to and including International, small tour level, sharing the training and riding. Nancy kick-started this book, so we are thrilled to bring it to fruition.
(September 2020)

Acknowledgements

Pammy and Islay wish to give special and grateful thanks to the following people, without whose help and encouragement this book would not have come to publication:

- To the outstanding support we have had from top professionals in many aspects of our sport, who gave time and experience so generously in all the interviews we conducted.
- To the photographers past and present, who have allowed us to use or reproduce their photographs to illustrate this book:
  - ∞ Kevin Sparrow (front cover picture.)
  - ∞ Bob Langrish MBE (Nick Skelton & Big Star)
  - ∞ Trevor Meeks (Mark Todd/Jeanette Brakewell/Jonty Evans)
  - ∞ Kit Houghton (John Whitaker-Gammon)
  - ∞ Emile Faurie Foundation website. (EFF photos)
  - ∞ Carole Payne for the other cover pictures and help with a huge amount of the structuring of this book.
  - ∞ Mary-Anne Horne and Stepney Bank Stables. Newcastle. (for EFF photographs)
- Brian Hutton and David Auty for endless patience, support and encouragement, especially with Brian's excellent critique and editing skill.
- Jill Day for her thorough and constructive technical criticism and some excellent ideas on adjusting the text to make it more appealing to the reader.
- Helen Needham, Ann Price, Kate Pritchard, Nina Boex and Rebecca Thomas for painstakingly reading the manuscript in entirety or at various stages of completion, making useful suggestions and corrections some of which had been previously unnoticed.
- To Emma at Talland, Emma who assisted in communication between Pammy and Islay on many occasions, managing the random 'bits' of text that flowed both ways between us.
- All the 'horsey people' to whom we mentioned the concept of this book for an opinion, which in general was enthusiastic and supportive to 'get it written'.

Foreword
by
Nick Skelton C.B.E.

Show Jumping has served me well but it hasn't come without 100% commitment and hard graft. The horses of course were the most essential part of my team but without owners there would be no horses of such great talent as those I've been privileged to ride and win with. And without the team at the yard, grooms and family, I couldn't have had the success I've had.

To get to the top in show jumping it is necessary to work your way up through all the levels of competition. It is important to find a good trainer, right from the early days, don't wait until bad habits have been formed which are then hard to correct. Both your own and the horse's. Competition at the lower levels is important, that is where the foundations are laid.

My favourite horses have always been horses who were "people horses", they liked humans and enjoyed interacting, making it easy to have a good relationship with them. Dollar Girl for example, she loved hanging out with the grooms at a show. And Big Star, he loves children, he is so gentle with them.

For all horse lovers from all disciplines and those who simply enjoy hacking out, this book will be a great read about the history of horses from "beast of burden" to how we got to where we are today.

"Where there is a passion for your chosen career then the days, weeks, months and years will fly past without you noticing. Each day will be enjoyable and it will not seem like a task."

Nick Skelton

Contents

Illustrations: Karen Mortimore

Professional photographs: Kevin Sparrow. Bob Langrish. Trevor Meeks. Kit Houghton.

Introduction

If you love horses, then this book is for you! If you have always loved horses, but never had the opportunity to get closer or understand why folk get hooked on horses, then read on - but beware horses are addictive!

WHY this book has been worth writing:
- For those of us who cannot live without horses in our lives, but for all of you that may be reading this book with a curiosity for why 'horses are for life' we thought we'd 'put pen to paper' and explore the obsession.
- From a seed of an idea, this book has turned into an exciting project of research and exploration.
- It will take you from a brief history of the evolution of the horse (not boring we promise, just informative) through the last 2000 years to the role of the horse in the 21st.Century.
- If you are a young professional, aspiring to progress through a fascinating and all absorbing career, where you will never be unemployed, then read on and be inspired by the personal accounts of what the love of the horse has ignited.
- If you want to know more about the amazing achievements of riders from all our Olympic disciplines and elsewhere, who have continued to ride at International level well into later life, when other top sporting athletes have long since retired from competition.
- It will be an innovative publication that will encourage reflective good practise, horse care and management. With critical analysis to deepen and enhance the knowledge of anyone involved with horses in whatever role.
- This book considers and celebrates the role of horses as our teachers.

WHAT you will find in this book:
- There are fascinating unique interviews from medal winning competition riders and others who have overcome unbelievable experiences in life, to form remarkable alliances with 'the horse'.
- There are interviews elaborating on how the horse has sustained his role as a much loved 'partner' in so many lives of those 'hooked on horses'.
- There is technical advice and opinion on the care and management of horses from some leading professional equine veterinary experts.
- We have highlighted some iconic horses that have become 'household names' for those of us that love the horse world. Their fascinating

individual partnerships formed with their riders, will enthral you with the depth of empathy established between equine and human, forming a life-long bond.

- There are many anecdotal accounts from both authors highlighting the uniqueness of every horse, the love developed between human and horse, and the sometimes humorous, situations we have found ourselves in with a horse.
- There are case studies giving genuine true insights into the role horses play, in the ups and downs of our lives.

WHEN you feel the 'bug' awakening your latent interest in the horse, the following delights can be explored:

- Once ignited, 'the love of the horse' bug is usually there for life. This book will show how it can 'come and go' through the ups and downs of life, but when you need it to sustain you, it can bring you joy, solace, recovery, rehabilitation, sanity, relaxation, friendship and longevity.
- We have included thoughts on life/work balance and keeping 'significant others' involved and valued, while you follow your passion.
- As a vibrant sport, e.g. Dressage, Show Jumping, Eventing, Racing, Driving, Polo and many, many other activities where horses are central to the partnership, this book will show the longevity of both the horse and the human equestrian athlete, which is unique to horse sport.

HOW will this book impact on you?

- The book will be a blend of youth and experience. The horse can be and is, enjoyed from babyhood to old age. Our Monarch in her nineties is the epitome of 'horses for life'. Still enjoying horses as a rider, owner, in sport, breeding and in every role, she simply radiates 'just loving them'.
- We will invite opinion on the role of the horse in the 21st century, the pace of life and returning to riding after a break.
- How can you deal with the intensity and pressure that working or owning horses, can sometimes become a threat to your 'love of the 'horse'?
- How can you enjoy or be involved with horses if you are not riding?

WHERE the horse plays a unique role in the many aspects of remedial work and therapy with children and adults, whose circumstances in life may have disadvantaged or excluded them from society.

- We have explored and applauded the priceless way that the horse enhances lives and in many instances facilitates a way forward, which could never have been considered before the introduction of 'the love of the horse' factor.

- We consider the continually developing role of the horse in transforming lives affected by disability or those disadvantaged by life.
- The horse does not choose to work with us, but his generosity to share our lives and expectations of him are often limitless, as long as we remember that he does not think like a human, nor is he hampered by our human emotions.

Dreamt up, thought out and produced by two educators! The **why/what/where/when/how** words in a sentence, we hope will promote thought and reflection. Our overall aim is to enhance and celebrate the unique relationship we have with the horse.

Understanding the horse in our lives w partner, which will ensure his welfare is of paramount importance.
This book is a cornucopia of indulgence in the love of the horse.

Chapters can be read consecutively or randomly, chosen in isolation. Throughout the book there are personal quotes from a range of successful equestrians, highlighting

their individual experiences and reflecting their 'love of the horse'.

Pammy and Islay are extremely grateful to everyone who has generously contributed and supported us in the writing of this book. We hope it will continue to inspire anyone who has a love and passion for horses.

PROFILE OF THE AUTHORS

We are of similar age (don't ask – it's nearer 70 than 65!!) and our paths first crossed literally some fifty years ago when we were both competing at the Amberley Horse Show.

This wonderful spring outdoor show was held on the Bathurst Estate in Cirencester and featured a wealth of equestrian competition, from Grade A Show Jumping to Driving and every conceivable type of Showing in between. Such outdoor shows were prolific in the 60s, 70s & 80s and were used predominantly for qualification for the International shows later in the season. Qualifiers for The Royal International, The Horse of the Year Show (HOYS) and Area International Trials (A.I.Ts) were confirmed classes at these shows and all the top riders of the day competed at them. Horses always competed on grass before the development of surfaces and indoor venues.

That early meeting was only really a crossing of paths as, even then, Pammy barely spoke to anyone when at a competition. Nowadays she would admit to shyness, but always trotted out the excuse of concentrating. As the years rolled by Pammy and Islay have become firm friends, and through writing this book have discovered that it should be of no surprise, as in their upbringing there were so many similarities.

PAMMY HUTTON. (née Sivewright)
My biggest aim is to help those with a huge passion for ponies and horses and, above all, a love, based on their own instincts and of course those of their equine partners.

I have to admit personally to no gold medals, although I have helped with the training of several who have gained a few. Had I known then, what I know now, I might have been closer myself.

The wonderful thing about horses is that one is always learning something. If one keeps one's eyes and ears open, then there is something to learn every day. Every horse and rider trying to form that partnership, starts on that learning, building trail.

There are many 'roads that lead to Rome' but the route based on common sense is the best.

I have to say that the single, most influential, person on all my horsey understandings and learnings was my mother, Molly Sivewright and her three books, Thinking Riding Book 1, Book 2 and Lungeing.

These books were and are a tremendous asset to every instructors' travels through the paths of equestrian understanding. I have never been much of a reader, as from a very early age I was taught to "watch those ears" and that appears a great deal easier.

My aim is always to pass on as much as I can, that I have learnt over the years and hope that some of it will guide another to the same deep love of the horse.

By the age if fifteen I was busy teaching, in those days there were no worries about insurance and qualifications, only the aim to pass on knowledge.

Growing up in a close family unit, the eldest of three daughters, loved by parents and grandparents, in a household where there were strict rules and parameters of behaviour, laid down by a Father who had served in the Army during the second world war.

My relationship with my Father was one of love, respect and some fear, we all heard about the War and it left me with a profound hope that World War three never happens. Father was a brave man, defying orders to go behind enemy lines to rescue his Sergeant. He adored my Mother. He was full of proverbs: 'look after the pennies and the pounds look after themselves' and 'a stitch in time saves nine'.

I went to a variety of schools as Father moved around with the Army and only passed five O levels and two A levels, but I did a secretarial course which I'm sure has been an asset.

We also learnt cookery which has stood me in good stead and I have never found it difficult to cook a meal for forty with little notice. My maternal grandmother was the cook of all cooks and taught me to use the Aga. My paternal grandfather was a very good Doctor, if apparently an interesting character.

I remained close to my parents all my life and it is challenging in this modern, frenetic, world to find time for relationships. (see Ch 9) We clock watch from the time we wake up and in this competitive world one can end up working around the clock.

Holidays taken in Cornwall were always special family times. Renting a house in Polzeath we would spend two weeks surfing, swimming, walking, reading, fishing, reading, playing cards, putting the world to rights. A time to share and unload stress and inevitably from time to time, family fights. Working out the priorities in life is always a challenge.

An enormous influence on my life, my Mother was fiercely independent and a workaholic. She devoted her life to my Father, to us and the development of Talland School of Equitation. This family run business was built around horses and the students we had, and still have, training there. She encouraged us to ride but it was never forced on us. All three of us competed on Junior European Teams and we all still ride, teach and love horses.

Her vision for training and development was way ahead of her time. She invited many of the top trainers of the day to Talland and I learnt through watching, listening and having lessons from Dick Stilwell (Show Jumping Trainer, although he helped with a Dressage team at the Montreal Olympics! There was much cross-discipline sharing in those days), Captain Dick Micklem (a brilliant horseman and Dealer based in Cornwall), Sheila Wilcox (3 times winner of Badminton), Major Bolternstern (Dressage Gold medallist), Dr.Reiner Klimke (6 Olympic Gold medals), Klaus Balkenhol. George Theodorescu, Harry Boldt, Conrad Schumacher (all renowned German trainers), Ferdi Eilberg (Germany/GBR) and more recently Moreton Thomson (Denmark) and Henk Von Bergen (Holland - International Dressage Trainer.). Of course, currently I watch Carl Hester - don't we all! He trains my son, Charlie, and I try to stay as current as I can with how our sport and industry is developing.

I have never paid a lot of money for any of my horses and trained all of them (around 14) to Grand Prix. There was a time in the 80s, that I worked in Italy, and it was there that I worked with Silver medallist Show Jumper, Vittorio Orlandi, and his best friend Mr.Nelson Pessoa (father to Rodrigo). We spent hours working on exercises on the flat to help the jumping horse.

My sisters both married and left Gloucestershire. I stayed at home and was lucky enough to marry my husband Brian, who also believes in Talland, and we have worked our whole life to maintain it, as my parents did for me.

We have a son and daughter, both of whom have also represented GBR at Junior and Young Rider level and my hope is that 'horses' will go into the next generation. Certainly at this stage it looks as if they will.

My Mother was pivotal in the development of the BHS exams in the early 1970s, with her leadership as Chairman of the Examinations Committee, she evolved the Stage Exams to develop a clearer pathway of learning, giving a stepping stone between BHSAI (Assistant Instructor) and the BHSI (Instructor) by creating the BHSII (Intermediate Instructor) qualification. Talland was, and still is, an Examination Centre for the BHS qualifications and needless to say I was directed to take the relevant exams, as and when the time came.

The BHS Fellowship is the highest standard of all round equestrian coaching competence in the UK, recognised world-wide, which I proudly achieved over thirty years ago!

Since 2000 the development of equestrian education through the Coaching Development Action Team (CDAT), established across disciplines by the British Equestrian Federation (BEF), has evolved a more enlightened delivery of knowledge, skills and competences, to reflect the range of learning styles that young people coming into the equestrian industry have come to expect through formal school education.

This broadening of delivery has led to the secure system of Coaching Certification now adopted successfully by the Olympic Disciplines and Pony Club and to a lesser degree in Vaulting and Driving.

Embracing the value of the British Dressage Coaching Certificate Level 3 and adding that standard to my repertoire of qualifications has undoubtedly enabled me to reflect more effectively and develop my training in a more rider led capacity.

I have competed all my life and was brought up being encouraged to win whatever game I was playing, but also to lose with grace and dignity.

I rode in the Junior European Eventing team in 1968/69 being placed 8th and 12th individually. My competitive highlight was being listed as travelling reserve on the Senior Dressage Olympic

team for Montreal, Canada in 1972. In addition, I won Windsor Three Day Event three times and was second at Punchestown, the latter giving me a longlisted place for the Senior Event team of the day. I am proud to have competed to International Grand Prix on over a dozen home trained horses.

Training achievements include Team Trainer to a number of foreign teams (half the Gold Medal winning Italian event team at the Moscow Olympics 1980, Italian National Horse Trials team 1982, Ireland for the European Championships 1983, Australia for the Barcelona Olympics 1992). Individuals include a number of Juniors, Young Riders, Senior Event and Dressage riders in addition to multiple Paralympic medallist Anne Dunham, (see ch 3) who inspired Suzannah Hext, who in her own right, has achieved Para European medals. (see ch.6)

I have trained countless individuals making their career in the horse industry, including my compatriot author for this book.

I still train and compete regularly, and we hope this book will open up opportunities to past and present riders, to see that age is no barrier to the lifelong enjoyment that we can have from horses.

§

ISLAY AUTY (née Dawson)
In August of 1950 our Queen gave birth to a daughter and in September of that year so did my Mother! I am a staunch Royalist and this close association to the Princess Royal through a fate of birth date just five weeks apart, has been a theme through my life, HRH as we all know, followed a path steeped in the love of horses and that is what I have done, although in a slightly different way to the Princess!

My Grandfather, Father and Uncle were all doctors and I was brought up in a very 'medical orientated' household.

My Grandfather and Father were both Consultants, specialising in Rheumatism and Arthritis at their private practice in a town in the middle of Worcestershire which was about as far away from the sea as one can get in England.

Maybe that is why I have always loved the sea and had a hidden obsession to live near enough to see it, smell it and hear it. An obsession as yet unfulfilled.

My elder sister and I grew up in a house invisibly divided into two halves. At the front of the house were two rooms that were known as the Consulting Room and Waiting Room, plus a small office and washroom. They were situated to the right of the front door overlooking the 'front garden'. During weekdays, when patients were coming to the house to see 'the two Doctors', (when both Doctors were consulting, the Sitting Room was used by my Father) the front of the house and the front garden were strictly 'out of bounds' for us.

We very quickly learnt as children that we should be 'seen but not heard'. We had a huge Great Dane dog called Wallace and my sister and I had to 'play quietly' with the dog in the 'back garden'.

I had no family background of 'horses', although my Mother had ridden a little as a child but had never been able to expand her interest, as my Paternal Grandfather was Chief Chemist for 'Shell petroleum' and the family moved frequently, both nationally and abroad.

My Mother always quietly supported my increasing love of horses. In fact, she managed to persuade my Father eventually to sell the Grand Piano that none of us played and that funded my first horse when I was sixteen.

We were a close-knit family and every Summer we went to Bracklesham Bay in Sussex for a month and it was there that I had my first riding experience.

A small riding school within walking distance of where we stayed, became the source of my ignited passion for horses. At the age of four I rode a small skewbald pony called Trixie and was instantly 'hooked'.

For three years the Summer months of July/August became the focus of my longing to ride more regularly. At the age of seven I progressed to regular weekly riding lessons at a local riding school in Worcestershire and my lifelong commitment to horses was secured.

As soon as I was independent enough to ride my bicycle to the stables, I spent all my time there, except when at school. I managed eight O levels and 2 A levels, it should have been three A levels, but I deliberately walked out of my Chemistry exam because I had no intention of being a Doctor (certainly my Father's plan for me). When the results came through and I had 'failed' Chemistry, my Father's anger and disappointment culminated in 'well what **are** you going to do?' and my answer of 'I'm going to work with horses' did not make his day any happier.

When you don't own your own pony/horse you ride anything that comes your way and I did.

Naughty horses, young horses, rides when the owner was away, too busy or losing interest, all came to me and helped make me the efficient, brave, determined, rider I still am today.

I would compete on 'anything' that I was offered or could 'beg, borrow or acquire'. Mostly Show Jumping in the days when the lowest class in BSJA (British Show Jumping Association) class was a 'Foxhunter' starting at 3ft 9" (now 1m 20)! These days the lowest starting class at an affiliated show is British Novice at just under 3ft (90cm)!

My bravery these days is tempered by knowing that falling off is not in one's interests and to be avoided by not riding lunatics!

I was a member of Pony club from the age of ten and, in spite of not owning a horse of my own until I was sixteen, I always managed to beg, borrow or hire a riding school pony to go to rallies and camps, although it precluded me from the 'team and competition' side of things.

I suffered a degree of discrimination over the fact that I was 'only mounted on a riding school pony'. As a riding school owner of later years, 'school horses/ponies' are absolute saints, they absorb the inadequacies of learning riders and are the animals that sustain the income and life blood of a riding school.

'School horses' without doubt fund the 'prestige/smart horses' that may be available for more competent clients or the competition horses of the school owner.

Over my years in Pony Club I attained all the progressive tests, including the still highly regarded A Test.

In the early 1970s riding was a 'hobby' and then one got a proper job! I soon recognised that to stay in the evolving leisure and competition horse industry (see ch.1.History) I must be able to earn a sustainable living.

The British Horse Society qualifications of Assistant Instructor. BHSAI British Horse Society Instructor BHSI and Fellow of the BHS FBHS were developing as recognised standards of competence of instructing riding/training and horse management.

That was my route to a future in the horse industry. I followed an intensive four-month course towards achieving the BHSAI (British Horse Society Assistant Instructor's Certificate) at the renowned Crabbet Park Equestrian

Centre in Sussex, run by Fellow of the British Horse Society, Brian Young.

Ironically, I wanted to go to Talland School of Equitation which was in Gloucestershire, closer to home, but my parents were anxious for me to be further away from home, to begin to develop more independence.

My first full time job was in a riding school in Sussex, followed by a two-year period in Canada. During those two years I worked with hunters and event horses. The family I worked for owned a beautiful property close to Montreal and in those days, it was the venue for the only three-star Three Day Event (now 4 star) held in Canada or North America. I was fortunate enough to watch at close hand, and sometimes ride with, the USA Event squad as they prepared for the impending 1972 Olympics (Munich) with the top Event trainer of the day, Jacques le Goff. The USA squad were based in the yard where I was employed for two months, prior to travelling to Europe. Two years in Canada enabled me to develop confidence, technical knowledge, competence as a rider and independence, both emotionally and financially, to then return home to train for my full BHS Instructor's certificate.

Seven months with Mrs Janet Sturrock FBHS fine honed the thoroughness and attention to detail, in both the training of horse and rider and the management of a yard, that ensured I could achieve the BHSI. Mrs Sturrock ran a small training yard in Rutland and was a fanatical member of the Cottesmore Hunt. She hunted every Saturday in the season. It was not unknown on hearing hounds on her property on a Tuesday afternoon, she would throw open the doors of the indoor school where a group of four or six of us students would be having a jumping lesson and say 'come on' (she was always mounted herself on a Tuesday afternoon!) We'd abandon the lesson and go and have an hour's hunting at the end of the day!

After gaining my BHSI in 1973, I then married my amazing husband David, who has steadfastly supported my passion for horses. He has given me a lifelong relationship of love and friendship and has never questioned my shared commitment to him and our son Robert, with my love of the horse and my career. (Xref: Ch 9. 'significant others' sharing)

From 1976 I spent nearly twenty years running a BHS Approved Riding School in Worcestershire with a business partner, also a BHSI, where we trained students, broke and schooled young and maladjusted horses, taught riders from 7 to 70 who were weekly riders, many with the same passion that I had and still have, for all things equine.

During this time, I was able to compete on a regular basis on home trained horses and for clients. I loved competing but it always took second place to 'earning a living', running a successful business and trying to do right by a tolerant husband and growing son.

I developed as a Dressage Judge (to current National List 2) and progressed through the ranks to become a Chief Examiner for the BHS, a position I held for some twenty-five years. This time included a spell as Chairman of the BHS Examinations Committee, the Training and Education Committee and a three-year term on the British Horse Society and BEF non-executive boards.

As the BHS examination system expanded, I was responsible for the writing of some eleven publications for the Society, documenting the examination levels and including 'Learn to Ride with the British Horse Society', the BHS Manuals of Stable Management and Equitation.

A variety of young horses that I bought cheaply, produced to Advanced Medium level Dressage, capable of jumping around an Intermediate Event and a Foxhunter level Show Jumping course before selling and starting again, ensured my continued personal development as a rider.

Running a BHS approved riding school in partnership for nearly twenty years, gave way to 'going it alone' and becoming a Freelance Instructor.

A degree in Education then followed, at a time when everyone seemed to be gaining a degree in 'something equestrian related'. I decided that since I had been 'teaching for twenty years the best thing for me was to validate my ability as an 'Educator'. It was without doubt a great decision, learning so much more about 'delivering' my existing technical knowledge.

With the achievement of the Fellowship of the BHS in 1995, a very proud moment, as my path to this acknowledgment of expertise had not been enhanced through high flying competition results, I attained a personal goal of continuing to be 'the best I could be'.

I believe (and can prove) that much of my knowledge, and then practice, has been achieved through 'watching' and I have always strived to listen and learn from many of the top international trainers who would come to the UK for invited seminars and conferences. Dr Reiner Klimke, Bert De Nemethy, and Kyra Kirkland, to name a few of the countless elite to whom Pammy has already made reference.

I have always been incredibly fortunate to continually access training from some outstanding trainers of the time (Dick Stilwell/Steve Hadley/Geoff Glazzard - Show Jumping) and (Brian Young FBHS, Pat Smallwood FBHS, Janet Sturrock FBHS, Molly Sivewright FBHS, Pat Manning FBHS, David

Pincus BHSI, Mike Garman – Dressage) but the person who supported and believed in me in my quest for personal achievement, and without whom I would not have achieved what I have, is Pammy Hutton.

Having been long term Coach for the Three Counties Dressage Group founded by Lorna Johnstone (XRef. Ch 3), her daughter, Nancy Nash, took over the Chairmanship on Lorna's death. Nancy and I had become friends through the Riding Club connection and for many years after giving up the Riding School, I was fortunate to be based at Nancy's lovely home in the lee of the Malvern Hills, where I rode and competed her horses. The opportunities Nancy gave me on her lovely horses led to our lifelong friendship and sharing of our love of the horse. When Nancy died from cancer in 2014 I lost a special friend and her generosity to me has led me to dedicate this book to her. Pammy rode one of her horses 'Excelssima' to international small tour level.

At a time when there were expanding opportunities in careers for youngsters wanting to 'work with horses', I became involved in the development of the UKCC (United Kingdom Coaching Certificate). This Government supported initiative funded the structure and delivery of sport technical competence, through a wide range of national sports.

Equestrian was one of the first of 22 sports to pioneer a validation of competence, which has become secure over the last two decades, to give the Olympic Equestrian Disciplines a recognised and respected qualification of 'coaching' the competition rider.

This qualification now independently endorsed through the awarding body 'First4Sport' and named for each of the Olympic Disciplines (e.g. BDCC - British Dressage Coaching Certificate) ensures that young people coming into a 'teaching career' in the horse industry develop the necessary skills of 'how to deliver' their knowledge and competence.

They then must tread the path that Pammy and I have resolutely trod for decades, which accumulates the vast wealth of knowledge that gives one the ever expanding 'tool box' of 'what to teach'.

Qualifications can often be denigrated by the 'those who can do' voice and 'those who can't teach'! I prefer to state that to drive a car one has to pass a 'driving test to show one's competence to a minimum standard of safety and ability'. One can then strive to become the 'best driver one can be in all situations' or one can flout the law, throw caution to the wind and become a liability to anyone unfortunate enough to meet you. As an educator one will often be judged by what you demonstrate and produce.

Countless young professionals have trained with me and are now earning their living in the horse industry, most of them with BHS and/or UKCC qualifications and within those, several Fellows!

For seven years I served on the British Dressage Board with responsibility for development of under 21 training and was also both Chef d'Equipe and Selector to under 21 International dressage teams from 1999 to 2014. I had been the Chef d'equipe to the first team to go abroad for an inaugural European Pony championships in 1976. The knowledge and experience I gained through all those periods of regular international travel with top trainers, both from home and abroad, was immeasurable, challenging, but amazing fun too.

I have many loyal Event and Dressage riders who have trained with me for years, through pony, junior, young rider teams to adulthood.

My highlights as a trainer to date have to be:

Working with a four star rider (now 5 star) at major Events such as Badminton and Burghley. I started training this rider at the age of twelve and she is now a well-respected, professional, producer of Event horses to all levels, in her own right.

Working with a rider competing on her home trained horses, now at Grand Prix (Dressage).

Working with a child who I first taught at the age of six and seeing her blossom into a successful young adult Event rider, now competing at 4* level and aiming 'to be the best she can be'.

The satisfaction that I achieve from 'starting' a person on their journey to loving the horse, is equally satisfying and certainly what **'gets me up in the morning'.**

These days one is encouraged to recognise one's USP (Unique Selling Point) and mine evolved through trial and error! The loss of my only sister at the age of 48 to cancer, was life changing for me and gave me a different perspective on life. Primarily it made me realise that there are no guarantees in life, and one must make opportunities and then seize them to maximise the value every day. It was one of the catalysts of my decision to leave the security but limitations of running a small Riding School

As a freelance Equestrian Coach my focus has been on youth development and also on coach education. These I believe have become my strengths and I care passionately about both.

I have been fortunate to travel to South Africa, Hong Kong and California, as well as Europe and Scandinavia, for around twenty years, with the remits of coach education and youth development.

As a coach educator my highlight was being invited to South Africa in 2007 to run a national coaching course for trainers from each of the provinces of South Africa.

Having written the British Horse Society books for the existing examination structure in the late 1990s early 2000s, I then expanded my repertoire with 'Coaching Skills for Riding Teachers', 'School exercises for Dressage and Jumping' then in 2016 I co-wrote the publication 'The Power of Coaching' with Penny Pollard (Director of Core Context - a Company specialising in the training and development of 'coaches' in Business).

I am riding as actively as I can and train regularly with Pammy, who continually motivates and challenges me. We have a common passion to bring our love and knowledge of horses to anyone of any age who might choose to share that commitment.

The years run away from us and we must maximise every opportunity for as long as we are allowed to.

I did not compete for around 12 years for a variety of reasons, including major back surgery on a badly prolapsed disc in 2000. For four years I stopped riding.

Realising recently that time is ebbing away, and I went into the horse industry because of my love and passion for horses, with the huge expansion of my knowledge and expertise over the last 18 years, why not put that back into practise and enjoy myself. Around 2015 I started riding again.

Pilates (see chapter 7) has given me a new and unbelievable flexibility and confidence in my fitness, suppleness, coordination and balance. I swim two or three times a week to complement my cardio-vascular fitness.

Returning to competition briefly again recently, has revitalised my awareness of 'what the rider deals with, in the competition arena'. That can only improve me yet more as a Coach and a Judge.

My son Robert is married to Kate, and they have given us two delightful grandsons, James and Tom. I watch the boys in a way I never had time for when bringing up my own son. They learn through 'curiosity' and through 'testing the boundaries'. Without bringing Social Services running around to challenge my 'grandparenting skills', I set parameters of behaviour in exactly the same way that one does with a horse or a dog. I have the children on a Thursday, they are delightful diversions from my day to day love and work with horses, but there are huge similarities in the confidence they show in knowing what is allowed and what is not!

Discipline instilled in youth in, my opinion, then facilitates the development of 'self discipline' which becomes a vital asset in all walks of life.

That life balance (see ch.9) is challenged but managed, so that we can enjoy the family and they us. Pammy talks about learning every day and I cannot finish my profile, without recalling words my Father spoke to me when he was well in his seventies and still practising as a Doctor. When we asked him why he didn't retire, his answer was: "when I don't wake up and want to be a better Doctor today than I was yesterday, then I will retire". I feel that same passion and drive and completely 'get' what he meant.

§

Writing our profiles individually has revealed some remarkable parallels. A strict but loving family upbringing, discipline from parents and home environment, work ethic, respect for others and a deep love of the horse from a very early age. For both of us, Grandparents who were Doctors. Great Danes in both of our lives (not the most common dog to own – sensitive, nervous and not long living). Pammy's Grandmother produced, and won three times running at Crufts, with a Great Dane and the trophy was awarded to her in perpetuity. Pammy trained her Grandmother's dog to 'go on the stage and lunge like a horse'!

Islay trained the family Dane to jump around a course of 'show jumps' on the lawn in the 'back garden'. Pammy suffered a broken back and the subsequent cumulative effects of that injury on her riding. (see ch. 6) Islay had back surgery for a badly prolapsed disc and has benefitted from pilates (see Ch 6) in her rehabilitation, to further her riding career in later life. Both valued the training from such greats as Dr Reiner Klimke (Germany), Bert De Nemethy

(USA), George Morris (USA), to name a few. It is little surprise therefore that this book has begun to take shape. We hope you gain as much from reading it, as we have in the collaboration of writing it.

CHAPTER ONE

KEY POINTS:

- Evolution
- Greece and Rome
- Medieval Times

- Renaissance
- 17th to 19th Centuries
- Post World War Two

WARNING:

This chapter requires a possible 'boredom warning'!

The contents are not for the faint-hearted. It is simply a factual account of how the horse evolved and became our life-long partner. It may be valuable if you are interested in how the horse developed to become our valued and treasured ally in war, work and now leisure. If you are aiming for the BHS Fellowship, then this may prove a useful resume of the horse's historical evolution and relationship with humans. If you are looking for a more light-hearted approach to the subject, then you may be wise to avoid this chapter and move on. It summarises the evolution and development of the breeding and training of the horse for the purposes that he has been, and is now, employed with us. For anyone needing a short version of the history of the horse then please read on.

HOW DID THE HORSE AND EQUESTRIAN SPORT EVOLVE?

The horse as we know him today has evolved over the past 45 to 55 million years. First recorded as a small multi toed creature about the size of a large dog, we now see an animal with a single 'toe' that ranges from miniature ponies around 60cm (-6 hands) to the 'heavy' horses who can stand 200cm (20 hands) or more at the shoulder today.

Approximately 5,000BC Horses were first used to transport man or his burdens. Probably horses were first used for driving. There is a record in the British Museum of a rein ring from a chariot pole of a Sumerian Queen (3,200BC). Historical evidence shows horses were used in Assyria, (now North Iraq and South Eastern Turkey) Persia (now Iran) and Egypt. From 1580 to 1320 BC Egypt has evidence of rudimentary types of bridle, so it is likely that horses were being ridden by this time. The huge grassy plains of Asia (now the Middle East) were well suited to the development of the horse for ridden purposes. Horses were ridden under constraint with a definite arch of the neck and a considerable degree of 'collection'. Evidence indicates much use of stallions, smaller than horses of today, but strong, short necked and stocky in build. There is little evidence of saddles being used although sometimes a type of saddle cloth may have been employed.

From the mid 700's BC chariot racing is recorded in Greece and by 650BC ridden races were also becoming more prevalent.

GREECE AND ROME

While the Greeks did their best to civilise the Romans with limited success, horses were used for transport, sporting spectacles of skill with horses, but often violence too and the hugely popular chariot racing.

In 430 BC, the Greek cavalry officer Xenophon was probably the earliest advocate of gentleness, natural training aids and no loss of temper. He wrote an Equestrian treatise 'Hippike', which still exists today. Xenophon wrote that it was the rider's responsibility to educate the groom in stable management and care of the horse. 'Hippike' clearly conveys pleasure in the relationship with the horse and its riding. This was in a time when the horse, as a companion in pleasure, let alone an object of affection, was totally alien. Xenophon advocated a multi jointed type of 'bit' acting like a chain in the mouth, this way the horse is constantly moving to find consistency in the mouth contact. The theory that through this looseness the horse 'lets go' and does not 'set against the bit', still holds good today. The horse will receive the bit more readily if something good happens when he takes it. Xenophon recognised the value of not coming back on the horse's mouth, especially when jumping. He therefore encouraged a position of the upper body above the hips to be upright and not behind the movement, with suppleness in the lower back, which alleviated fatigue for both horse and rider, and enabled a more secure seat (less likelihood of falling off!). This position is not reflected in the portrayal of riders on coins and vases of the period, which show riders sitting back with legs and feet pushed forwards.

The Greek culture of the time was entering a 'golden age of enlightenment,' where art, literature and philosophy was developing to heights never previously attained. Riding reflected the civilisation of the period; schooling of the horse was gentle and enlightened.

Alexander the Great, 330 BC, also showed gentleness with the riding and training of horses during his era.

Saddles and stirrups, all came to Europe from Barbarian invaders from the East, followed a little later by horseshoes. These Eastern nomad invaders rode with free extended paces and control with the voice was encouraged. The saddle and stirrup probably originated in China and early saddles are recorded from the Fourth Century AD. Byzantines brought them, copied from Eastern Barbarians, and stirrups in the Sixth Century AD, from the Huns of Attila.

After the Fall of Rome, (mid 1400 AD), mounted cavalry became increasingly important. The system of 'Roman Roads' that had been developed throughout the strength of the Roman Empire provided easier travel, horses were encouraged to 'pace' (a two-time smooth gait without a moment of suspension), which made riding much more comfortable.

MEDIEVAL TIMES

Charlemagne increased the use of cavalry and he hunted on horseback. During the following medieval period horses became valued possessions but only as a means of transport. The development of heavy armoured knights required the breeding and development of much heavier horses to carry the weight of the rider.

Standards of equitation began to recede from the enlightened age of Greece and the grandeur of Rome. A period of cruelty ensued, sharp rowelled spurs were employed, as the knight's legs were encased in armour and nowhere near the horse's side. Strong curb bits were used to attempt to turn, or stop, the bigger, coarse horses quickly. Crusaders in close contact fighting began to suffer from invading Saracens, who came from the East on lighter, agile, more mobile, steeds of the Arab type of breed. These gradually began to infiltrate Europe. The development of firearms saw the end of the armoured knight and jousting remained only as the sport of the nobility. To date, ability to ride was regarded as a God given gift which was the heritage of noblemen.

The stage was set for the development of serious schooling and riding as an end in itself.

RENAISSANCE.

In the early part of the 16th Century a development of schooling horses evolved which was different from anything previously. There were three Italian trainers of note: Grisone, Fiaschi and Pignatelli. The Neapolitan School was founded by Grisone, who wrote about the importance of the use of the rider's leg. Fiaschi wrote about the use of circles in the basic paces, the development of collection in canter and the high school 'airs'. Pignatelli founded his own school and became the most famous horseman of the period. He attracted horsemen from all over Europe, who came to study. Two French riders, De La Broue and De Pluvinel, took the ideas back to France and exerted great influence on the developing era of horsemanship in France.

At this time the Spanish School evolved, and it is not entirely clear whether it was an offshoot of the Neapolitan School or established as an independent parallel. Spanish riders and Spanish horses started the school in Imperial Austria which still exists today: The Spanish Riding School in Vienna.

Early school riding was very 'collected' involving methods of restraint with horses 'behind the bit' with the nose well behind the vertical. No extended or free gaits, nevertheless these were huge steps and the foundation (especially as the French school developed) for Dressage riding and training of today.

The Neapolitan school existed for four centuries however its ascendancy was short lived. The reasons probably could be given as emigration of experts to other parts of Europe. There were many internal disputes in small principalities in Italy and perhaps the Italians were temperamentally unsuited to training difficult horses at that time.

The French Court and the Imperial Court of Austria were a grander stage than the warring Italian principalities. The type of riding in any country at any period reflects the interests, aspiration and civilisation of its people at the time.

Some years before the birth of the Neapolitan School, Leonardo Da Vinci studied and wrote about the 'proportions of the horse' and invented the 'hand' as a means of measuring the horse.

17th to 19th Centuries AD

This period was probably the most important era in the development of equitation and the methods of schooling became the foundations on which we still rely today.

The focal point of 'classical schooling of the horse' had moved to France.

De la Broue wrote the first book on Equitation by a French Author and he speaks for the first time of developing schooling according to the horse's character, physical development and ability. He defined *'good hands', as 'knowing when to resist and yield with good timing and receive with precision the action produced by the legs.'*

He was one of the first to mention jumping and he was an advocate of cross country riding to educate the horse to expect the unexpected.

As a result of the success of De la Broue and De Pluvinel, Louis X1V supported the new movement in Equitation and the school of Versailles grew and flourished. France also began a selective breeding programme of horses in the Royal Studs. De la Guerinière, while not a direct pupil at the School of Versailles, was 'a disciple by osmosis'. He became the most important link to the 'golden age of academic equitation', he was an innovator and brought equitation into modernity. His book 'Ecole de Cavalerie' filled the gap left by the School of Versailles, as no technical testament was left to the time of Louis X1V and Louis XV.

The three great lessons that he evolved, the shoulder in, half halt and acceptance of the aids, represented the culmination of the period. The joint effect of the shoulder in and the half halt is conclusively tested by 'the horse on his own, without recourse to the aids, must maintain the position given to him by the rider and continue to perform the movement begun without any alteration'.

De la Gueriniere became the 'patron saint' of the Spanish School in Vienna and the French master's book became their 'bible'. An enduring cult also devoted to De La Gueriniere perpetuated through Germany.

The school of Versailles was the name given to the whole philosophy of French Court equitation. Saumur was founded in 1771 and the Cavalry School there was re-established in 1814 under Louis XV111.

While major development was taking place in France, similar progress was being made in Germany. The Germans followed De la Gueriniere ,with Gustave Steinbrecht being the major link with De la Gueriniere's teaching to his home country.

The Scandinavian Countries were producing competent riders and trainers, which reflected the corresponding development of equitation in these countries. Sweden and Denmark particularly were keeping pace with the evolution of equestrian training in Europe.

In England, Fox Hunting became the increasing influence of riding and in the mid 17th Century much of equestrian life revolved around the country squire or local nobility but there was not the concentration of nobility that revolved around the court of France.

There was some infiltration of Neapolitan teachings from Italy through an enlightened scholar and nobleman, the Duke of Newcastle. His own education and horsemanship was of a high order and he maintained the methods followed by leading continentals of the time. However classical riding waned after the exile of The Duke of Newcastle to Holland when Charles 1 was deposed. Hunting was well established by the 18th Century. The collected horse of the manege, with the rider in an upright position and long stirrups, was not suited to hunting so the rider's position changed, and horses were encouraged to become fast and uncollected.

The 19th century horseman was mounted on superb horses, riding with courage and often athletic ability but with a total absence of sound technique. Military equitation prevailed as the horse became pivotal in the role of the Cavalry. The evolution of the English Thoroughbred, from influence of Arab and Turkish blood, led to the creation of the General Stud Book introduced in 1791, hence the beginnings of the sport of Racing in England.

In late Victorian Britain, there were still in the region of one million working horses on farms and working deliveries in teams such as brewery dray horses.

From the mid nineteenth century steam power was taking over the role of the horse in transport and agriculture. Working teams used for brewery delivery became an increasingly rare sight.

Hundreds of thousands of horses were requisitioned for the First World War, where they were used as mounted cavalry, supplies, mounted scouts and ambulances. The war had a devastating effect on the horse population in Britain and only as a result of **dedicated horse lovers** were some of the native breeds maintained.

THE ROLE OF THE HORSE SINCE THE SECOND WORLD WAR.

Post war Europe saw the strong development of breeding programmes for the production of the 'modern' sport horse. Germany, Holland, Denmark, France, and to a lesser degree the Scandinavian countries, all have a well-respected breeding and grading system for recognised sport horses. Iceland and Finland both have a 'pure' breed of 'cold blooded' horse that has evolved as a work 'heavy' horse. The Finn Horse has been developed successfully into a utility horse for dressage, jumping, trotting and general recreation while staying 'true' to their historical origins. The Icelandic horse similarly whilst staying a pure breed is renowned for its five gaits including the 'tolt'.

Britain has developed its strength in the breeding and development of the Thoroughbred for Racing, and to a lesser degree the Event horse still with a major influence of the Thoroughbred or Arab 'blood'. Racing is the second largest spectator sport in GB and generates huge revenue in the industry overall, and through betting.

Recreational use of the horse has now prevailed as the major role of the horse in modern life. Horses of all types and breeding work in riding schools, trekking and trail riding, riding holidays, showing, hacking and companions. Breeding has a great emphasis for sport in all disciplines, but especially the Olympic disciplines of Dressage/Show Jumping and Eventing. Horses also fill a vital role in the lives of those who are disabled (physically or mentally), those disassociated in society, those with communication problems (Autism or Attention Deficit Hyperactivity Disorder-A.D.H.D.) and those who have been alienated from society. Horses in the lives of many can enhance their life quality and provide rehabilitation that often cannot be found easily elsewhere. (ref Ch.8)

GB excels in all the Olympic Equestrian Disciplines and as a Nation we maintain a magnificent range of horses from native ponies to Olympic superstars. All add to the ongoing development of the horse in 21st Century Britain.

It is estimated that there are around 1 million horses in the UK, with 19 million equestrian consumers in a range of associated interests. *(Source British Equestrian Trade Association)*

There are in the region of 60 million horses worldwide, with the largest concentration in the United States of America.

REFLECTIONS:
It can always be valuable to consider the 'history' of a sport or a subject of interest.

The background of the origins of the horse can provide insight into how and why our use or working with this wonderful creature has evolved.

Past knowledge can often prevent us from making the same mistakes that our forefathers made.

Irrespective of where we live in the world, the horse remains a herbivorous herd animal who thrives more mentally and physically, when living in a group rather than in a solitary state.

The horse is a horse the world over, the differences in how we treat him depend on our culture, our climate, our beliefs and values in our upbringing and our history.

The latter point is the reason this chapter is included.

SUMMARY:
History of anything enables us to know 'from where things originated', 'why things were done in a certain way' and 'what has already been tried or done before'.

Some knowledge of the evolution and development of the horse within the global development of mans' progress, may ensure we do not try to 'reinvent the wheel' in the management of the horse as our partner in life.

Congratulations if you have reached the end of this chapter! You now have a summarised knowledge of how the horse evolved and how he has become the equine we know today.

CHAPTER TWO

WHERE IS THE BEGINNING? - where does our love of the horse come from?

KEY POINTS:
- Origins
- Innate
- Acquired
- Instincts
- Feel
- Empathy
- Head or heart

ORIGINS

For those of us that have withdrawal symptoms if we do not see, smell or touch a horse regularly, one can wonder where that obsession starts? It is wholly understandable for families whose background is steeped in horses, that the offspring of such families will automatically be drawn into the same environment, that ensure horses become part of life.

It may all start 'at the beginning', every child should read 'Moorland Mousie by Golden Gorse' pseudonym for author Muriel Wace and the more famous 'Black Beauty by Anna Sewell', the latter a literary classic, there are probably comparable modern publications. Exposure to these kinds of literature, create the early learning so vital to those involved with any animal, but here specifically directed at the love of the horse. Surely we all need passion, caring, kindness, softness and the ability to express honesty in life, especially to those with whom we share our lives (human or equine)?

One has only to look at the Whitaker 'Show Jumping' family (XRef Ch 3) to see the 'dynasty' that has evolved, with almost every member of the family being involved in some way with the horse. Similarly, in Dressage there is the Eilberg family where Ferdi, himself a successful Olympian, has then fathered two prolifically competent riders, who have both represented GBR at World Class level, and one son who follows another career, in spite of them all growing up in the same environment. As our authors' profile will remind you, we evolved from one 'horsey family' and one completely 'non horsey' background. The Sivewright family were steeped in horsemanship and this has followed through the generations into Pammy as an International rider/trainer, and now her two offspring who have followed in the family tradition. The Bullen family, similarly have delivered four generations of 'horsemen', Jane Holderness Roddam (née Bullen) Olympic Gold medallist in Eventing, Jennie Loriston Clarke (née Bullen)(X Ref.

Icons Ch3) World Championship medallist and multi Olympian/European team member in Dressage. Jennie's daughters, Anne and Lizzie respectively, and granddaughter Charlotte, have all represented GB in Dressage. What is it that switches on that passion and then sustains it through the rigours of a physically and mentally demanding relationship with the horse, not to mention the time and huge financial commitment that horses dictate?

Consider alternatively 'programming' the child into a specific sport? Andre Agassi (World Number One Tennis player in the late 1990s) was 'committed to tennis' from a very early age by a highly ambitious father (ref: Andre Agassi's autobiography – remarkably he professes to have hated tennis for his formative years.) The Williams sisters (Venus and Serena) were also directed by their parents into the intensity of training and development that is necessary to produce champions. Similar to tennis, swimming, athletics and gymnastics require certain criteria of mental and physical ability, identified in youth, and with a clear structure of coaching and development, to determine a fairly reliable outcome. In other sports it is possible to identify potential 'athletes' to train for a specific activity.

The hugely successful multi medallist in Rowing, Dame Katherine Grainger, was identified at University to have the physique that would facilitate her ease as a Rower. She was then directed through a talent development programme which was specific for her sport, her becoming GB's most successful female Olympic medallist was the outcome.

Not so with riding. Riders come in all shapes and sizes, they may be introduced to a pony before they can walk, or they may have no access whatsoever to an equine, then when finances and family allow, they take up riding in mid or even later life. Gymnastics would rarely be a sport that was taken up in later life.

Children who 'grow up with a sport' are generally fearless until they hurt themselves. The old saying 'you have to fall off seven times before you are a rider' may convey resilience and confidence on the brave committed child, but the first time of falling, can also be the last time they choose to ride. It is likely that the offspring of a 'horsey family', for whom falling off is just another part of 'home life', having watched parents or siblings have falls, will build resilience and a 'c'est la vie' attitude to falls. A child without that example of 'accepted normality', may find it more difficult to manage. Islay's experience was that her parents were keen for her to 'pass the horsey stage' as soon as possible, so whenever she went home having 'hit the deck' there was an element of 'that's fine if you don't like falling off, give up riding'. How much that increased Islay's resilience and determination to get better and fall off less, was obviously completely underestimated by her parents!

Few sports can claim seventy-year old Olympians; and riding is one of the rare sports that one can take up at any stage of life. The benefits to one's health, both mental and physical will be explored and the well known saying by Sir Winston Churchill **"there is nothing as good for the inside of a man as the outside of a horse"** rings very true. Horses through good management and increased veterinary developments are now able to compete successfully into old age. A horse is a horse the world over, whether it is a thoroughbred racehorse, a Shire heavy horse, a Shetland pony or a Polo pony. It is the same warm-blooded, herd animal who is a herbivore and creature of flight not fight. It is the culture, climate, history and way of life of its owner or breeder that dictates how its type is developed and trained. Of course, a racehorse cannot be trained to fulfil the role of the heavy horse and vice versa, but the mind of the horse whatever its breed, is the same whatever its end role will be. If we forget that, the partnership between horse and owner will be inhibited.

The authors have been involved with horses all their lives. Inevitably that conveys a level of knowledge and experience accrued over the nearing seven decades that we have enjoyed our partnership with horses. There is value in highlighting the developments of training horse and rider, the management and treatment of horses over this time. . We learn in a huge range of ways,

29

but if we have any chosen opportunity, we learn from experience. Experience is that illusive quality that you achieve about five minutes after you need it! On a horse, or with a horse, that can often be uncomfortable or at worst painful.

So, we should learn from others who have been through the experiences that we wish to access. In other words, we can learn from those more senior to us, those with a wide range of life events and in this case those with experience of horses. With wisdom however, we can also learn through the vibrance, uninhibited curiosity and courage of youth and this is often overlooked.

We might think we know it all, but in fact where horses are concerned, we almost certainly don't. Horses learn completely differently to us, if we do not accept that fact and 'be able to think like a horse', we will never develop that true partnership of love, trust and empathy that is one of the greatest delights of sharing the relationship with a horse. Horses learn from repetition and memory of a pattern of behaviour or treatment. They do not share the emotional involvement and reasoning power that contributes to many of our thought processes.

In general horses cannot gallop faster or jump higher than seventy years ago. There are huge advances in veterinary diagnostics and care, plus the ancillary services such as physiotherapy, chiropractics and osteopathy ensuring increased longevity in the competition horse and of course in us the rider. We intend to highlight some of these later in the book.

This has to be one of the few sports achievable to Olympic and International level by many. We are lucky enough to have gained personal knowledge and fascinating unique interviews from some of these riders, to include within these chapters. We so hope that what we have learnt will get some of you out of your chairs and onto the back of a horse for the first time, or back to riding if you have let it lapse. It is never too late to live the dream and not only dream the dream.

INSTINCT:

Dictionary definition of **Instinct**: An innate, typically fixed pattern of behaviour in animals in response to certain stimuli.

Dictionary definition of **Impulse**: An involuntary prompting to action. The natural impulse by which animals are guided, apparently independently of reason or experience.

To stand quietly and just watch your horse or pony, without him noticing that you are there, is an art in itself; if you sneak up some how they always hear you! You have to quietly but naturally approach, they probably do know that you are there, but will not change their attitude in any way, and that is what you are hoping for. This will tell you far more here than rushing for the thermometer or the stethoscope. This also means no running up to the box, shouting enthusiastically "Donald, Donald, how are you today, shoo, move over, and wake up" etc! It really does mean, without being overly noticed, just quietly observe.

Is your horse standing up or lying down? If they are lying down is it because they are sleeping comfortably, or resting but awake? So little is understood about animals by some of those living close to our stables, that we receive several telephone calls a year informing us that one of our horses has died in the field. Often a horse will lie flat out in the day if the sun is shining and will sunbathe! If they are lying down, most probably it is happily relaxing. Once a horse has a routine, they will probably switch off at the same time each day, or night. If they are standing up, each horse will have a particular way of resting. He may rest one hind leg, and then the other; he may rest a front leg forward and out, although this could mean pain in the foot, as it is not always normal. Some horses however do rest diagonal pairs quite naturally, so we really do have to spend time just watching, in order to understand what is normal and what might not be.

After posture, we need to observe whether his ears are forward, resting slightly turned outwards, or pinned back. Forwards is an indication of 'happy', although it can mean 'looking', slightly turned outwards 'listening', back can be 'anger' or 'pain'. Sometimes one can be forwards, and only one ear 'listening'.

The ears, eyes, nose, mouth, and tail will tell you everything your horse is thinking, and linked together with his body posture, will tell you all you ever need to know about his moods.

We feel that the art of watching a horse is really a missed opportunity in today's modern world, and this very simple, yet all telling method, is often left untaught. There is also the art of listening to him breathe. One can only envy those with far more experience than us, who just stand and listen to a horse and can tell that his lungs are great, or that he is in need of a good gallop, and this is before they listen to him on the move. Again, this ability only comes with listening and watching many horses. If you hear one cough and it is immediately followed by a sneeze everyone can relax, no sneeze, and one goes on cough alert!

Islay recalls riding one of Nancy Nash's horses (to whom this book is dedicated) who would cough and sneeze for the first few minutes of sitting on him to warm up. His nose would be at floor level as he stretched his whole frame in 'this early morning clear out'. If he didn't follow this habit we were concerned that all was not 'normal'.

Pammy recalls two of her most favourite people to have into the yard were Dick Stillwell, and Captain Dick Micklem. The latter was Colonel Sivewright's best friend, and the former a world-class Trainer. They would just sit on the mounting block, and watch. By the end of the day Pammy was informed which horses were worth keeping and which ones were to go, and sometimes which ones would go of their own accord unless...! "Pamela; get that one's heart listened to" was right on the button.

The ailments are many. What we have to remember is that horses were never designed to stand in their stables for twenty-three hours out of twenty-four, and so we must try to mirror nature on as many occasions as possible. This starts with understanding how our horse feels by just watching and listening. Is he depressed, fresh, in a bad mood, hungry, lonely, tired, or just peacefully at rest. Watch your horse early in the morning, sometimes at a quiet lunchtime, or later at night. Pammy is lucky enough to sleep within earshot of the yard, and at night reckons that she can hear a horse that is even slightly upset, by the different night-time sounds. It is easy to hear one that is stuck (cast) in his stable, and years of listening to the signals, to realise that one of the horses is not right.

Pammy firmly believes that 'feel' dictates fifty percent of the results in the competitive field through stable management; after all, if the horse is not feeling right, how is he to perform at his best? It is a worry that there are never enough hours in the day to spend enough time with the horse, off his back. It is one of our constant resolutions to make and break. "Time" is a commodity that in this modern day and age of instant coffee, tea, and computers, runs even faster, but there is no 'instant' horsemanship! Oh! How one wishes for more hours in the day. Attention to detail, to every detail is a must. It is always easy in hindsight to realise before a big day, "Well now I think about it there was a little heat in that leg".

Pammy recollects fondly a conversation with the great racehorse trainer Sir Henry Cecil. "If you have two equally talented runners" Pammy asked, "do you know which will win?". "Ahh it's all in the slippers!" came the answer. Sir Henry went on to explain that very early in the morning of the day of an important race, he would go quietly into the yard (in his slippers!) and just watch the horses, he would glean from those moments of quiet, before the day began, what kind of night his horses had had and the tiny fluctuations in behaviour that might be relevant for the day, or in the future.

We keep a book in the tack room and write down any differences that occur, that way if something does go wrong it becomes easier, with reference, to understand even more quickly what might be going on. Even keep a chart every day and pencil in the work the horses did and how they performed. This can help you to understand what type of pattern of work can bring about a win. Charts and records are vital. It is no good having a feed chart up if it is not a current record of the food that the horse is receiving, and maybe this sounds a daft statement, but with a yard full of more than ten horses, how often one hears "Yes, that is the food that Wilf is getting, except for the extra late night that his owner Mrs Neverwrong suggested". Or "I just thought that he seemed a little fresh with you today, so I cut his food in half". The result takes several days not hours! This is, of course, if one is unlucky enough not to be able to do the feeding ourselves.

The most important saying in feeding is still the old one of; "the eye of the master maketh the horse grow fat." There are some that one leaves the feeding to, who have different ways of interpreting sizes of bowl - heaped or rather meagre!

At this point one of us had better admit to still having a yard of nearly 100 horses, and the irritation of not being able to do everything ourselves. We can also admit that as much as we love the training of the horse, so do we love training and working with people, young and old, who have a will to learn. It does not matter if the person wishing to understand horses has come from the middle of a town with no experience of horses. It is all in the keenness of that person, the desire to learn and the **love of the horse**, and it is our intrinsic belief that "**dedication**" is the most important word of all!

So often in the stable management of the horse, the day-to-day care of the horses will fall on to someone who is training, and less experienced than perhaps we are. So, the next most important word is **honesty,** and this is a hornet's nest! Here we need, "No, I am sorry, but I forgot to give Wilf his late-night feed," or similar, and let us tell you from experience that honesty is not a modern word! It is vital when winning by a mark or losing by a second relies on attention to detail, and that detail is honestly worked at by all those concerned.

Another thing learnt, which is based on the importance of watching, is that when buying a horse, look at how a horse looks out through the door, look at that head, and the expression, and ask yourself whether you will give it stable room for the next twenty or so years! It is important to try to turn up early when viewing a horse that is for sale, as you are more likely to catch him less set up, more natural. One can receive lessons on how to make a horse look one thousand pounds more expensive. Presentation when selling seems to be the key here! So, when buying, turn up early! A horse can be taught to put his ears forward, and how to stand him up to look more valuable, again the posture is all important, but here we are moving on to man made, and at this point we are still interested in what is natural, to the horse.

Almost everything we do to the horse is unnatural to him.
We put him in a stable for hours on end, we clip him, put rugs on him, put iron on his feet, make him up a mixture three or four times a day that resembles our breakfast cereal. We put metal in his mouth, a thing we call a saddle on his back, give him a bed that takes some guesswork to remind us of nature, and dried grass which we proudly call hay! If this horse is successful, we then cart him halfway around the world,

with travel sickness drugs at the ready! If the horse is really good at Jumping, we ask him to trust us enough to throw himself over drop fences, gallop over or into water, jump up to seven feet in the air, over poles that do knock down, but should be left standing. We want him to race at speed over fences or to go slower for long distances – maybe that is preferable! However, if the horse moves well, we do 'dressage' with him, and apparently all the movements can be seen done quite naturally out in the field! We are still looking for that field!

So, all in all we feel that we have a duty to scratch our heads every minute that we spend with our horses, to see if we can remain as close to the natural as possible, whilst balancing this with the extra that we need to do to them to gain results. Pammy recalls a horse that went successfully around Badminton. This was achieved from him living out in the field. He was allergic to practically everything in the stable, and his way to show his distress was to box walk, which did his legs no good at all! So often one would wish that horses could talk, but as you get to know each and every one, they all communicate with us in their different ways. This comes from a lifetime of experience, and maybe our first ponies suffer a little, but Pammy was lucky, with parents who both had special relationships with their four-legged friends along the way, and from this stemmed her own passion.

FEEL: The dictionary definition of is:
- To perceive by touch.
- To be conscious of.
- To be keenly sensible of.
- To know by touch
- To have the emotions excited.

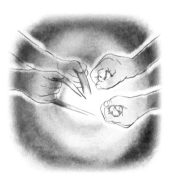

Touch is one of the 'senses', and for an able-bodied person it is something we 'take for granted' from an early age. Learning hot from cold, hard from soft and from these basics, the danger of 'very hot or very cold' and hard or soft that could injure us; e.g. knife or water.

Sensitivity as a rider is fundamental to the communication with the horse. E.g. contact through the rein may vary tremendously depending on the level of training of the horse, its breeding, type and the way it has been trained to accept the contact, however the hands holding those reins need to be sensitive enough to 'hold the reins firmly and consistently enough to stop a baby bird flying away, but sensitively enough not to squash it!

At the World Equestrian Games in Kentucky, USA in 2010, it was a blind rider who informed the organisers of the Games that the International Dressage arena was short by one metre (normal size is 20m x 60m)! How incredible, that it was a rider without sight, who was able to impart this information. Close your eyes for a few seconds (or minutes if your balance and coordination allow) and you will discover how dependent you are on your eyes to stabilise your balance, as well as to inform you when and where it is safe to move. A blind or partially sighted rider will have developed their other senses, especially **feel**, to counteract the lack of sight.

Feel therefore is an invisible quality that every rider should be striving to enhance, to further facilitate their communication and harmony with the horse.

The rider develops **feel** through the security of the basic riding position, stability through a supple lower back and level seat with even controlled weight influence in contact with the horse's back. A feeling rider is a more effective rider, developing awareness for the predicted or unpredicted reactions of the horse and moving as one with the horse.

An understanding of the scales of training of the horse through:
- Rhythm/Relaxation.
- Suppleness.
- Contact,
- Impulsion.
- Straightness.
- Collection.

Will enable the rider to coordinate their influence, through correctly applied aids, in timing with the balance and energy created from the horse.

Understanding basic horse psychology will further facilitate the harmony between horse and rider. The rider must be able to 'think like a horse' so that they are able to identify with the reasoning behind tension and resistance from him.

Relaxation but reaction, is a fundamental requirement for good training of the horse and as these qualities become more secure, the horse's 'submission' to the rider's communication, becomes seamless and imperceptible. Sensitivity between horse and rider then becomes more highly developed, the physical and emotional connection between the two beings becomes evident as a vision of total symmetry in the performance of the partnership.

Feel is like any other skill, there will be varying natural ability in a rider, but some will have to work harder at developing feel than others. Any skill needs practice and consistency to improve. In a rider, the perfecting of feel comes from the improvement of the basic correct, supple and deep seat, to develop a balanced ability to move with the horse. Various exercises can then be employed to develop awareness of when the horse is moving each limb, when a hind leg is not under the horse in support, or when one limb works more efficiently than another. The rise and fall of the horse's back under the seat can be identified in all three paces. The clarity of a hind leg 'pushing' into a canter transition or making a flying change is a further aim for the rider to feel. Repeating transitions with guidance from an 'eye' on the ground, will help to confirm your opinion of what you are feeling. Mirrors can also assist in your observance of 'what is happening under you' in comparison to your **feel.** As your **feel** develops, so will your timing and aid application, assuring a greater harmony in the partnership with any horse.

For those of us who are fully 'able-bodied' how fortunate are we? Ask a disabled rider who has one or more limbs missing, a sightless person or a paralysed person what they '**feel**' and the answer will be very different from our perception. Through this humbling experience however, we can and should develop more 'empathy' to expand our understanding of **feel.** This can only benefit both those we teach and the horse. Many a trainer will say 'you have **feel**' or 'did that **feel** better?', or 'did you **feel** that?'. What is our answer? We may not know what we are meant to be feeling, so we say 'yes' to the question and continue in our fog of ignorance hoping for a 'light bulb moment of understanding'.

The horse can certainly help in our quest for feel. Tension or resistance, even small signs of ears easily forward or ears anxious and beginning to turn backwards, can give an early warning sign of further tension and resistance to come. If we 'feel' good, we ride better, if our horse feels good, he goes better.

How many times do we hear or say 'I was just thinking about you' when a person contacts us (phone, text or email). Yes, telepathy is an interesting subject too, but not for now. There are good feelings and bad feelings in us and our horses, we must work hard to 'bank' the good feelings to gain increased harmony with our horses. Some of the greats we will mention in this book have 'feel' beyond comprehension. As an example, Sir Mark Todd picked up a 'chance ride' on 'Horton Point' when owner Lynne Bevan was injured, they then won the premier 5 star Event in the world – Badminton in 1994. A partnership formed by Mark with a horse he had ridden only a handful of times.

Our development of feel should come from hours of riding different horses, frequently without stirrups or even bareback. Yes, we still do! Study those people who 'have it'.

A great horseman/woman, who are they and how did they become great? Islay remembers one Junior/Young Rider European Championships in Denmark 2010. It rained for the entire five days of competition, the stands were uncovered and were mostly empty. Sophie Wells MBE, (multi World/ Olympic/European medallist in Para competition), was contesting her second European Championships as a member of the Young Rider Team. She spent the entire competition (when not riding herself) sitting in the stand watching. Little wonder that her outstanding successes continue to accumulate. She still is the only rider to have represented GB in able-bodied and Para dressage teams.

Talk to any 'great', in any field of work, they will always tell you it 'has taken a lifetime' to become 'great', and rarely do they see themselves as 'great'.

A philosopher recently responded with passion to the Interviewer on 'Desert Island Discs', who asked why he continued to study and learn, although he was well into his seventies? He said, "I've spent a lifetime learning and I'm so skilled at it now, why would I stop doing it?". Pammy and Islay share that passion and sentiment.

EMPATHY: the dictionary definition is:
- The power of entering into the feeling or spirit of something and so fully appreciating it.
- Understanding and sharing the feelings of another.

- Showing emotion, affinity or sensitivity.
- Ability to sense others' emotions, 'feel'.

One might consider that all we have written on 'feel', can also be defined as or overlap with 'empathy,' in which case there is little more to add. We will avoid unnecessary duplication and repetition. Suffice to say that instinct, feel and empathy are fundamental terms that should be a constant thread through any relationship with any horse. They are characteristics that are intrinsic in the horse as an animal (wild, neglected, abused, misunderstood or trained), and they are characteristics that we need to develop as positively and effectively as we can if we are to have harmonious and confident relationships with horses.

We are as we are today because of our upbringing, our heritage, what we have learned within our lifetime and what we do with those experiences. We have learnt so much from those before us, so now try to remember to respect and listen to the 'older generation'. While youth is vibrant, forward thinking and wanting to 'reinvent the world', we do remember what that 'feels' like as we remember our youth, it seems like yesterday! As we get older, we reflect more: What if? Should I? Did I? Can I still? Reflection becomes an ever more valuable and self-motivating tool.

The word in the 'Empathy' definition we should highlight is **'sharing'**. We are sharing our love of the horse, with the horse; it is our choice not his choice. It is up to us, through our superior knowledge and reasoning to be able to develop empathy with the horse and **share** experience with like-minded colleagues to always enhance the understanding of 'our work with the horse'. Talking always helps. Sharing and talking resonate through many of the issues that this book highlights.

HEAD OR HEART

We often hear the reference to being ruled by 'your head' or 'your heart' and this is worth a mention here, in how we empathise with the horse.

Ruling with our head involves drawing on the rationales that may be in place through the learning or 'programming' that conditioning has imposed on us.

Ruling with our heart will usually relate more to the 'gut feeling' or 'instinctive' thought (or lack of it), that enables us to react more instantly.

The latter reaction is how the horse predominantly will behave. If we are riding across the beach, with the wind in our hair, the freedom and lack of constraint which that environment would generate, we are able to ride in harmony and partnership with the horse. We just 'do it'. Put the same horse and rider within the confines of a Dressage or Show Jumping arena and often, they so overthink a movement or fence, that they make a mistake which would not have happened in the unstructured situation. We must strive not to allow the head to overrule the heart.

Islay's account:
In a recent conversation with Pammy, when I was struggling with riding one-time changes on one of her long-suffering Grand Prix horses, I complained that I was not quick enough! She asked me if, when I cook, do I generally use a recipe? "no" was my reply, "I just do it". "Well stop over thinking it", was Pammy's quick response, "just ride a straight line and move your legs!". Amazing – result! I was so busy over analysing technically what I should do, that I failed to give the horse the basic information, which the horse clearly understood without my "overloaded thinking".

REFLECTIONS:
- Understand the horse's psychology. Avoid giving him human emotions, he has different levels of reasoning to ours.
- Understand the horse as a herd animal (not solitary), who thrives on eating (grass), running away from things that frighten him and having none of the emotions that tend to overwhelm us.
- Ask yourself to 'think like a horse' frequently. He works from memory; you work from intelligence (generally!).
- Your horse's memory is probably longer than yours! Ensure those memories are good.
- The most important way of communicating with our horse is through our brain, it is what we think or feel that is mirrored by the horse. Oh yes 'our moods show through'!
- Work tirelessly on developing instinct, feel and empathy. All these qualities will enhance the relationship and understanding you have with any horse.
- Fortunately for those of us who love working with horses, they will never thrive in a totally technological environment. The horse should thrive and benefit from our liaison with him.
- Strides in modern management can be embraced however and can greatly enhance the way we keep the horse in the working situation, where he is our partner.

SUMMARY:

- This is not just, 'another book about horses'. Our aim is to help those with a huge passion for horses already, (or a hidden one waiting to get out!) to indulge in that love of the horse based on their own instincts and, of course, that of the horses and ponies.

- Where does your love of the horse stem from? Do you have a family background, or was it introduced to you as a 'skill worth developing'?

- We all need passion, caring, softness and kindness. We need the ability to express honestly to our horses and this comes from asking yourself often 'if I were the horse would I understand everything that was asked of, or done to me today?'.

- **Instinct** is something many of us have for animals in general. As a horse lover one usually also has an affinity to dogs, cats or other animals. Many 'animal lovers' will profess to a better relationship with their animals than with humans. (X.Ref. A.P. McCoy – Champion Jockey - quote in 'Power of Coaching'.)

- **Feel** is fundamental to the harmony we aim for with horses, it takes practice, timing and an emotional involvement.

- **Empathy** is sharing and understanding the emotions of another.

- Ask yourself again: 'If I was a horse would I understand?'

- This book is being written in the hope that even one really keen person wanting to win that gold medal can learn something from the wealth of experience that will be revealed.

- It is also to show that 'we are never too old' and good exercise (and other life management) with our fabulous friend the horse, aids us in our quest to enjoy life for longer.

- If you have always wanted to ride or know more about horses and never had the opportunity, it is never too late.

- Let your **heart** rule your **head**, please read on and enjoy.

CHAPTER THREE

ICONS OF OUR SPORT

KEY POINTS:
- Show Jumping
- Dressage
- Eventing
- Para Dressage

- Unique interviews with John Whitaker MBE.
- Sir Mark Todd.
- Jennie Loriston-Clarke MBE
- Anne Dunham OBE.

This chapter will explore the longevity of some of our equestrian athletes in the Olympic Disciplines from all over the world, in able-bodied and Paralympic sport, also touching on other exceptional examples of equestrians, who have continued at the top of their sport much later in life than in any other sport. While athletes may continue to carry out their sport into old age and deserve huge merit, they are not setting world records for their speed, e.g. Marathon runners in their 80s.

The first 'icon' highlighted here, won an individual Olympic Gold medal (surely every athlete's dream of ultimate achievement) at the age of 58. Some individual interviews with well known equestrian 'names' add a personal and deep insight into what drives us to have horses in our lives.

SHOW JUMPING:
Nick Skelton CBE (dob: 30.12.1957)
Nick was given his first pony, Oxo, when he was only 18 months but the pony being exactly the same age as Nick it was a few years before he started riding Oxo. After leaving school with no qualifications, he went to work full time for the legendary riders and trainers Ted and Liz Edgar (née Broome). Nick won Individual Gold at the Junior European Championships in 1975 and in 1978 he set the British high jump record of 7 feet 7 inches (2.3m) on Lastic at Olympia, a record which has yet to be beaten. In 1979 Nick made his debut in a Senior British team and he became an integral part of teams for the next three decades. After his split from the Edgars in 1985, his successes on a number of top horses continued until September 2000, when a fall resulted in a broken neck and ended his show jumping career. Nick retired in 2001 but through sheer determination, after visiting several surgeons in Europe, he returned to riding and started competing again in 2002. At the age of 54 years Nick was part of the Olympic Gold Medal winning team at London

2012. After London, Big Star won the Grand Prix at Aachen in 2013 but that was to be his last win for two years due to injury. Four years later, with a replacement hip for Nick, and a rejuvenated Big Star, the partnership won Olympic Individual Gold at Rio 2020, Nick at the age of 58 years. Nick and Big Star finally retired together in May 2017 at the Windsor Horse Show at a memorable ceremony in the presence of HM The Queen. Nick's name is linked to many of the most outstanding show jumpers of the last forty years and his successes are well documented. From 1978, when he first won the Leading Show Jumper of the Year on Maybe, through to 2012 when he was a member of the British Gold Medal winning team at the London Olympics, then to continue with his vision and passion to Rio in 2016 when he won Olympic Individual Gold on Big Star, Nick has thrilled lovers of show jumping with his skill, dedication, resilience and determination. He is an inspiration to countless young riders who will continue to have him as their role model. For anyone who loves equestrian sport and Show Jumping in particular, the memory of Nick riding first in a four horse Olympic jump off at Rio, for the Gold medal, will be forever etched on us as being one of the most exciting, spine tingling, thrilling and emotional spectacles we will ever have the privilege to watch.

John Whitaker MBE (dob: 5.8.1955)

John has enjoyed a hugely successful career over four decades. (X.Ref. Ch 2) He has been a member of the senior British Show Jumping team for as long and has produced countless top horses. The most famous partnership being with the grey horse Milton, who was produced as a young horse by the late Caroline Bradley. His medal haul at Olympic, World Games and European Championships is over 20 and he has won every major trophy and championship in the sport.

Islay was fortunate to share a unique conversation with John's wife Clare, which revealed some fascinating personal thoughts about this outstanding horseman.

Q: What is John's goal now?

A: To continue to compete successfully for as long as he can.

Q: How and why did your children follow you and their Father into the sport?

A: They grew up on the farm where there were always ponies around and as children they played 'cowboys and indians'. They joined the Pony club and were involved in mounted games, they were always competitive and it just went on from there.

Q: What is the best thing about the involvement with the horse?

A: It's healthy, with the children growing up, I always knew where they were, and they were 'at home' in a safe environment.

Q. What is the most frustrating thing about the involvement with the horse?

A: It's full on 24/7.

Q: What has changed over your decades in the sport?

A: The fences, materials and the course construction have changed radically. There is much more money in the sport, both in the prize funds and in the prices of good horses. It is possible for a naturally less talented rider to achieve, if they are financed with good horses. If a less gifted rider always rides top quality horses and they have the determination, they can become good, but it always takes hard work, dedication and commitment whether you have natural ability or have to work at it. Riders are much more aware these days of the need to be athletes and lead a healthier lifestyle (not so much booze and junk food!).

Q: Which horses have been the most special?

A: There have been so many, but Ryan's Son of course was the first to project John into the top echelons of the sport. Milton was incredibly special and could have been an Olympic horse if the Olympics of Seoul (1988) had been closer to home. The Bradleys who owned the horse, understandably, did not want him to travel so far. Then there were Welham, Granouche, Hopscotch and Gammon, (X.Ref Ch 4) to mention just a few. They all won some phenomenal classes and John formed a formidable partnership with all of them. All his horses are special.

Q: Which was John's most memorable win?

A: European Champion at Rotterdam on Milton in 1989

Q: What are John's hopes for the future?

A: To compete at another Olympics and to win.

Q: Which has been the oldest horse to compete and win at top level?

A: Gammon won the Hickstead Jumping Derby at the age of 21.

Q: What is the key to keeping them happy at the top level of the sport?

A: We use road work, hacking and general consistency of fitness. We don't over-jump them, especially once they know their job. Keeping them fresh and happy through a variety of their work. (X.Ref Rachel Murray. Ch5)

Q: Does John have a favourite quote?

A: Keep trying'.

Michael Whitaker (dob: 17.3.1960.)
Younger brother of John, Michael has followed his elder brother into the 'hall of fame' of Show Jumping success. He became the youngest winner of the prestigious Hickstead Derby at the age of 20 (this record only overtaken in 2019 by the teenager Michael Pender aged 19), and has spent over forty years at the top of Show Jumping both nationally and Internationally. His medal tally at Olympic, World and European level is currently 15 and still competing at World class level, no doubt Michael's quest will also still ultimately direct towards Olympic glory.

Anneli Drummond-Hay (dob: 04.08.1932.)
This remarkable horsewoman has records as long as her arm! She still holds the World record for Ladies World Puissance (High Jump) of 7 feet 7 1/2 inches (2.36m). Winner of both Badminton and Burghley 5 star Events, the Hickstead Jumping Derby and European gold medallist. While still forging her competitive career in the UK, before emigrating to South Africa, Anneli was trained by Mrs.Molly Sivewright (Pammy's Mother). She is the only rider to have been selected for all three equestrian disciplines at the same Olympics and has represented both Great Britain and South Africa. She spent a brief time in the Netherlands training show jumpers, but her home since 1972 has been South Africa. She is quoted as saying 'I wasn't born to be cold'. While no longer competing at the highest levels, nevertheless this lady in her ninth decade, still rides up to five horses a day and competes when she feels like it. She states that "riding is like brushing your teeth, why would you stop doing something you have done all your life?". Anneli is most associated with the great horse 'Merely a Monarch' who was not a Thoroughbred, his grandmother was a Fell Pony and the pony blood made him intelligent. Anneli remembers him as a 'freak' of his time. He won Badminton and Burghley but was also a Grade A Show Jumper. An outstanding example of 'horses for life'.

EVENTING:
Sir Mark Todd: (dob:1.3.1956)
This eventing New Zealander is without doubt a 'legend in his lifetime'. Multi talented, having competed at World Class level in Show Jumping as well as Eventing, where he has won consecutive Olympic Gold medals in Los Angeles 1984 and Seoul 1988, Badminton Horse Trials four times (when winning in 2011 on Land Vision he became the oldest winner of the

event) and Burghley Horse Trials five times. In addition to Gold medals at World championships, 'Toddy' has competed in seven Olympic Games. At 6ft 2in (1.9 m) Mark's Olympic Gold medal winning ride in Seoul was the diminutive 'Charisma' who measured just 15.2hh (157 cm). In 2000 Mark was awarded the title: 'Rider of the Century' by the FEI which seemed to be a fitting way to round off a lengthy and outstanding career. Mark retired from International Eventing and returned to New Zealand, where he was involved in breeding and training, both Event horses and thoroughbreds for Racing, his horses enjoyed success in both fields.

Few could have imagined that after eight years, Mark would return once more to base himself in the UK. He competed in the Beijing Olympics 2008, returned to full time eventing in 2009 and went on to win Badminton again in 2011 on NZB Land Vision, 31 years after his first win. At the 2012 London Olympics and Rio in 2016 Todd became the second oldest New Zealand Olympian in history. Representing New Zealand, Mark Todd's medal tally is outstanding: Two Individual Olympic Gold, one Bronze, Team Silver and two Bronze (6 Olympic medals in total), Individual silver, two Team Gold and one Bronze at World Games and four Badminton, five Burghley wins and seven Olympic appearances with 28 years between the first and last Olympic medals! If ever a sport proved longevity that record certainly confirms it.

Islay's interview with Sir Mark revealed the following fascinating facts:

Q: What drives your passion?

A: The **love of horses** and the love of competing. Challenging yourself. The thrill of competition. Now in racing, my passion is success driven. To be riding a winner or now to be training that winner.

Q: Which has been your most memorable win?

A: Probably the first time I won Badminton in 1980 on Southern Comfort. I had brought the horse to England from New Zealand when I was 23 years old and virtually unknown. Mark Phillips was favourite to win on Columbus that year and when I won there was a cartoon in the New Zealand press along the lines of HM the Queen asking, 'Mark who?'

Q: Was this your most important win?

A: Probably as it 'put me on the map' and everyone started to know about me as a rider. I am probably remembered most for the two Olympic wins on Charisma because to win back to back Olympics on the same horse is still fairly rare.

Q: What drove you to return to the sport after an eight-year break?

A: I think it was the challenge. When I retired the first time, I had lost some motivation. I then had a few years in New Zealand in the 'doldrums' and people started to say 'go back to Eventing', I said 'find me a horse' so they did! I got my motivation back and a good sponsor in New Zealand Bloodstock. It was all dependent on the horse 'Gandalf' passing the vet, he did, and we qualified for the Beijing Olympics.

Q: What is the best thing about your involvement with horses?

A: They are just the most incredible animals, all have different personalities and the key to success is understanding them.

Q: What is the most frustrating thing about them?

A: Their unpredictability, one never quite knows what they might throw at you. I find the tricky horses challenging though and it is fun to find the right key to those. I learn from every horse. The little changes in them, the stable they live in, their reactions in the field, their 'relationships' with other field companions. In racing it is more a numbers game, with less involvement with the one to one relationship. I enjoy knowing the horses as individuals.

Q: What is your opinion about the change in the sport of Eventing from 'long format (including roads, tracks and steeplechase endurance) and the short format now used?

A: It has changed the type of horse that is required to be competitive, so the breeding and training has changed too. It's a different sport now. There are less injuries and horses last longer. Horses need to be better prepared and they need to be trained for the more technical questions asked from the courses. Previously, in long format, they just needed staying power and to be brave. There needs to be more attention to detail in all aspects of the preparation of the three phases.

Q: Which is the oldest horse you have competed at top level?

A: Campino was 16 years old when he won Burghley and I was still competing him at 17 years old.

Q: Which horse has been the most special?

A: Charisma. He was 16 when he won his second gold and that put me into a rare category only recently matched by Michael Jung.

Q: Do you have any regrets?

A: No regrets, I've met and worked with some great people, I've worked with a great team of committed people, had amazing owners and incredible support throughout my competitive life.

Q: What is your favourite quote?

A: 'She'll be right'!

Islay's feeling, after the telephone interview with Sir Mark, was one of complete euphoria that she had spent half an hour in candid conversation with one the greatest Event riders the Sport has ever seen. She has judged him on many occasions and obviously seen him countless times in the flesh at competitions and on television. To be actually involved in a one to one discussion with him left her 'on cloud nine', inspired and captivated by the passion he delivered in every answer.

Andrew Nicholson. (dob: 1.8.1961.)
This New Zealander moved to England in the 1980s to further his career as an Event rider. He remains phenomenally successful as a producer of horses and has won consistently at International level. He has competed in six Olympic games, winning medals in both Team and Individual competitions at World and Olympic level. He has won Burghley Horse Trials five times but until 2017, in spite of completing Badminton 36 times, the trophy had eluded him. That pinnacle of achievement (after Olympic Gold), which every Event rider aims for and dreams of, eluded Andrew until in the latter part of his career achieving that goal in 2017 riding 'Nereo'.

DRESSAGE:
Jennie Loriston Clarke. MBE.FBHS.
Jennie has been a leading figure in the development of dressage in the UK for the last 50 plus years. She represented GB at four Olympic Games (Munich 1972/Montreal 1976/Los Angeles 1984/Seoul 1988) won a Bronze medal at the World Dressage championships held in the UK in 1978. Awarded an MBE for services to Equestrianism and holder of the Fellowship of the British Horse Society (FBHS) she was awarded the first Queen's award for Equestrianism in its inaugural year of 2006. The Catherston Stud still headed by Jennie and husband Alistair with family support from both daughters Anne and Lizzie, is still a leading centre for the breeding and training of both horses and riders of the future.

Islay interviewed Jennie for a fascinating half hour, where she spoke from the heart about her own personal development as a rider from early childhood.

Q. What drives your passion for horses?
A. From a very early age I was 'stuck on a pony'. First a grey pony called 'Kanga' and then 'Darky' trained by my mother. We all rode (brother Michael Bullen, sister Jane Holderness Roddam (née Bullen – winner of

Team Gold medal at the Mexico Olympics in 1962 in Eventing), we went hunting with our parents often twice a week. I graduated from a safe pony to 'Skippy', the more I pulled the higher he jumped!

Q. Which was your most memorable win?

A. In the early days, winning the Winston Churchill Trophy at the Royal International Horse Show (RIHS) on Desert Storm, and also riding a horse owned by Mrs. Babe Mosely called 'Highland Fling', who was a Middleweight Hunter and won many championships because he was a big moving, expressive horse with four white socks and always gave a good ride.

Q. Which was your most important win?

A. Winning a Bronze medal at the World Dressage Championships at Goodwood in 1978, on Dutch Courage. I was trained by Ernst Bachinger and Dutch Courage could get quite tense, so Ernst sent me up the gallops at Goodwood before I worked in. Obviously, it did the trick!

Q. What is the best thing about your involvement with horses?

A. They don't answer back! They are so rewarding to train and I love teaching animals, which comes from my Mother who trained all our ponies to 'do stuff'.

Q. What is the most frustrating thing?

A. These days I don't ride much, so not being able to get on and show someone is the most irritating.

Q. How has the sport changed?

A. Dramatically! The quality of horses, the paces and movement that the modern horse has means the riding has to be more knowledgeable and effective. The production of horses, breeding and training on the whole is better. Horses have much more athleticism and impulsion. These are all changes for the better.

Q. What is worse?

A. Detrimental training of the horse, e.g. Rollkur, (defined as hyper extension of the horse's neck often associated with force or excessive pressure) and money, which can corrupt of course and sometimes result in a horse getting into less than competent hands, when its welfare is then compromised. There must be care not to overdo impulsion at the expense of tension.

Q. How old was your oldest competition horse?

A. It takes at least 4 – 6 years to train a horse to Grand Prix, then you hope it will improve and consolidate for about 8 years. Horses are often lasting longer these days through better management and veterinary methods.

Most of my horses continue to compete into their late teens. After Dutch Courage my horses have all been home bred and trained.

Q. Which horse has been the most special?

A. Dutch Courage of course, and Dutch Gold, who won the Midland Bank Championship (Eventing Championship) and then the next day went to Rotterdam to compete in a Grand Prix Championships.

Q. How do horses run in the family?

A. Father was in the Military and hunted. Mother trained ponies and dogs for Circus. My brother hunted and was a 'clown', and my sister and I Evented and I went on into Dressage.

Q. What is your favourite quote?

A. 'Give the horse the feeling to breathe forward'.

Richard Davison (Dob: 20.09.1955)

Richard is a four-times Olympian and has been at the forefront of International Dressage for four decades. He would be regarded as one of the world's most experienced International riders. He has been on the organising teams for many of the world's high-level competitions including World Cup qualifiers and European Championships. He is much in demand worldwide for his skill and experience as a Coach.

Hoketsu Hiroshi, Japan (Dob: 28.3.1941)

This Japanese national competed in his first Olympic Games in 1964 in Show Jumping. A retired Pharmaceutical Executive, he moved to Germany in 2003 to follow his passion of Dressage and train towards Olympic Selection. He competed at the Beijing Olympics 2008 (equestrian sport held in Hong Kong) and then again at the London Olympics of 2012. At both these Olympic Games he was the oldest athlete. He was aiming for Rio in 2016, where he would have gained the record for the oldest ever Olympic competitor, but sadly the horse was not fit enough so he withdrew, leaving the record in the hands of the late British rider Lorna Johnstone (see below)

Lorna Johnstone MBE (4.9.1902 – 18.5.1992)

Lorna participated in three Olympic Games, 1956 – 1968 and at the Munich Olympics of 1972. she became the oldest ever British competitor, and the oldest ever woman to take part in an Olympic Games. Lorna continued to ride well into her eighties. Nancy Nash to whom this book is dedicated was Lorna's daughter. Nancy groomed for Lorna at the Munich Olympics.

Ulla Hakanson, Sweden (dob: 9.11.1937)

This International Dressage rider from Sweden rode in her first Olympic Games in Munich 1972. She was a Bronze medal winner there, and again in Los Angeles 1984. She competed again for Sweden in the 1988 Olympic Games in Seoul 1988.

In September 2019, over thirty years later, this equestrian athlete competed at Falsterbo International Dressage competition on a horse called 'Diddy Cool'. Competing on this 12 year old horse that Ulla has bred and trained herself, their combined age was 94 and rising!

Her first international success came in 1970, and now entering her sixth decade of competing at the highest level of Dressage, her competitive record is: six World Cup appearances, 10 European Championships and six Olympic Games. She rode as a child, with a Father who was in the Military and has throughout her life embraced the love of the horse, being involved in Show Jumping before specialising in Dressage. This lady shows no sign of changing her commitment to horses in her life, in spite of some health set backs. She wholeheartedly reflects, fulfils and embraces 'Horses for Life.'

Carl Hester (dob: 29.06.1967)

Carl is still far too young to be included in this chapter because of his age! We are however unable to continue in this book without reference to this phenomenal man, whose 'love of the horse' shines through in every aspect of his work in equestrian life. He has without doubt revolutionised the attitude and approach to the management and training of the horse since his emergence into the industry at the age of 19, when he moved from the island of his birth (Sark in the Channel Islands) to Hampshire.

Between 1985 and the current day Carl has achieved success after success in his meteoric rise to become one of the most admired and outstanding trainer/riders of all time. We are extremely proud that he is British. He is a personal friend of Pammy, Islay is proud to know him, and he kindly wrote the foreword for her previous publication co-written with Penny Pollard - The Power of Coaching.

PARALYMPIC DRESSAGE:
Anne Dunham OBE

Islay drove to Wiltshire to meet Anne, spending a captivating two hours with her discussing her life with horses, and amazing development to become the holder of six Paralympic Gold medals in Para dressage. In her career as a

Para dressage rider between 1994 and 2016, Anne accumulated 19 Gold, plus several Silver and Bronze medals, winning 32 medals in total. What a huge privilege to chat to this self effacing, down to earth, horsewoman whose passion in life has so clearly always been 'the love of the horse'.

Q. Tell me a little about how your 'love of horses' started?

A. I was born a 'Lunn' in Northumberland and the first pony to take my attention was the milk pony, 'trot-trot' were some of my earliest words. Dad's work moved us South to live on the outskirts of Epping Forest. The first time I rode was at the age of 8 years with an organisation called 'The Horse Rangers of the Commonwealth. It was a bit like the Girl Guides and was aimed at those who could not afford their own ponies. I remember we wore green shirts with a white lanyard. It was founded at Hampton Court and I think HRH The Princess Royal was Patron. There is still a group based at Hampton Court. I absolutely loved it, we rode one week and worked for stable management badges the next week, alternately.

While living in Essex I rode at Pine Lodge Riding School in Epping Forest. It was run by Roberta Stone (now Bullman) who became my first riding instructor, a supporter and life-long friend. By the time I was thirteen years old I was helping to teach the younger children at the riding school, and by the time I was 16 I was taking out rides of up to 22 riders into Epping Forest. At the age of 18 I went to College in Newcastle, to train as a Primary School Teacher.

As a youngster on family holidays I volunteered daily to help with the beach ponies, I just loved to be with the ponies. Towards the end of College, while home on holiday I met Mervyn Dunham, who rode and owned a garage. He also played golf and loved to hunt. We used to ride out together at Pine Lodge. Early on in my time with Bobby (Roberta) she went on a course with Pat Manning FBHS, at Fulmer Riding Centre. Here she learnt about the Classical style of Horsemanship. We used to ride in a 'hunting position' with the leg forward, leaning back. The classical style had us sitting upright and central on the horse. This fed my desire for knowledge and I read all the classical books like 'The Complete Training of Horse and Rider' by Alois Podhajsky, who was a trainer of the Spanish Riding School in Vienna.

Q. Tell me about the development of your Multiple Sclerosis?

A. By the mid 1970s I was beginning to experience some balance issues and loss of limb coordination, particularly my right leg was failing me. The diagnosis of my condition was pretty muddled at that time and one Doctor even told me to go away and have a baby. In 1976 I did have a child, Amber, a girl came along. Sadly for all of us, the pregnancy seemed to further accelerate the onset of my disability and in 1981 I became wheelchair bound. I was thirty.

One of the side effects of my condition was extreme fatigue. I got tired easily and could no longer teach full time. I began to specialise in the teaching of reading to children who had learning difficulties. It was the time when conditions such as Dyslexia and Autism were being studied, children often slipped through gaps and struggled to keep up.

Q. What about horses during this time?

A. Although I didn't ride for five years, I still had much contact with horses and I still taught. There wasn't much I couldn't do in my wheelchair. I could muck out if I had to and certainly teach easily. I never let my disability hold me back and volunteered with the local RDA at Albury in Herts. By the 1980s RDA was introducing dressage tests and during this time Mervyn bought me a Side saddle. Someone in RDA had suggested that I would be able to ride side saddle, so we found an instructor and I learnt the skill. It is so comfortable and the 'leaping head' pommel makes it feel very secure. I continued to ride side saddle for several years.

We moved to Wales and lived on Hazelwell Farm, Whitland where we ran riding holidays and gave lessons. Amber became an excellent rider and all three of us would compete frequently over Cross Country, etc. As my condition deteriorated, I came to concentrate on Dressage. On the farm we had a small flock of sheep which we moved on horseback with the aid of a rescue sheepdog, 'Mac'. We took customers to Pendine Sands, where we could gallop along eight miles of beach. We had around 28 horses and 40 plus sheep. For a while I was Chief Instructor to the Vale of Taf Pony Club and Amber was having much success in the competitions we did. Then we went through a bad patch, where a number of negatives created a downward spiral. We had to sell the farm. All this had a bad effect on our marriage, so Mervyn stayed in Wales, Amber went to University and I moved to Wiltshire

Q. How did the para-dressage evolve?

A. I had leased stables at Dauntsey in Wiltshire, where I took liveries and trained a few people for their BHS exams. I was competing in the RDA Dressage Championships successfully on my daughter's horse, 'Star'

and during this time I was selected to represent Great Britain in several International Para competitions. These contests had the competitors riding borrowed horses. The horses were selected for the class by the Host country and the riders were matched by a draw. This was carried out on the first evening, the horses' names came out of one hat and the riders' names out of another. Then off we went! Sometimes we could take our own horse to ride in the 'own nation horse competition'. Two competitions I particularly remembered were at Hartpury in 1994 and European Championships in Portugal in 2002.

Para dressage was being promoted around the world by Jonquil Solt, who was a Director of RDA. She encouraged 24 countries to run international competitions for riders with disabilities. By 1996 it had become a Paralympic Sport and the first Paralympic equestrian games followed the able-bodied Olympic Games in Atlanta, USA that year. I was selected along with Pat Straughan, Jo Jackson and Elizabeth Jackson to compete. Our team Manager was Ro Pudden, and team trainer was Diana Mason. We rode borrowed horses and I drew a 13hh chestnut pony called 'Doodlebug'. He was completely overwhelmed by the enormity of the atmosphere as he had never seen anything like it. He was scared and unpredictable and when it came to the Freestyle to Music, I used music that had been put together for a horse with a much bigger stride. The challenge was to finish with the music and make it look like the music had been made for him. We did finish with the music and won an Individual Bronze medal. Great Britain came home with Team Gold and Individual bronze.

Para dressage continued to grow, in 2000 the Paralympics were in Sydney, Australia, when we still rode borrowed horses. The pony I drew was called 'Charlie Brown', he too was 13hh and I came home with Team Gold.

By Athens 2004 Paralympics came of age, and we took our own horses. I achieved team Gold competing on Ali Mills 'Orlet'. Beijing 2008 Games I took a naughty Welsh Cob called 'Teddy Edwards' and we came home with Individual Gold, individual Silver and Team Gold. For the London Games 2012 I was first reserve for the team but was not needed, so did not go, much to my chagrin and disappointment at a home Games. At Rio 2016 I was selected on Lucas Normark, owned by the Lady Joseph Trust and Henrietta Cheetham. We came home with 2 Individual Silver and Team Gold medals.

Over the years I have also competed in 4 European Championships, 4

World Equestrian Games and at many other International Championships. Horses literally took me all over the world.

At home my trainer was Pammy Hutton of Talland Equestrian Centre, Cirencester. It had always been my dream to have a lesson from the great Pammy Hutton at Talland and this is Pammy's version of how it came about.

Pammy account: *"Anne Dunham booked a lesson with me and, in those days, I'd had no experience of teaching riders with disability. I told my secretary that I would not teach Anne, as I did not have either the experience or the patience. Anne did not ride with me on that occasion. After a few weeks, Anne rebooked at Talland, with me, using her maiden name. I looked at my daily list seeing 'Anne' as a new client – not 'Anne Dunham'! I was advised that 'Anne' wanted to ride a horse that could teach her flying changes and she was mounted on 'Querqus', a chestnut gelding then working towards Grand Prix. When I entered the school, Anne was already mounted. Initial introductions progressed into the riding session and I mentioned that Anne's right leg seemed to be less effective than her left leg. 'Oh yes' was her reply 'lazy right leg, I was born with it'! The session developed and Anne rode flying changes for the first time!*

Anne says: "I didn't tell Pammy I was in a wheelchair and, until the end of the lesson, she had no idea how disabled I was. From then on Pammy became my trainer, friend and mentor and I owe much of my success to her help and commitment".

To continue the story of how Para dressage evolved, we need to address 'Classification'. The International Paralympic Committee (IPC) is the Governing Body for all Paralympic sports. They look to keep competition as fair as possible between people with differing levels of disability. A grading system is used, where the athletes are examined by 3 independent people (physiotherapists, chiropractors or others with medical expertise) to assess the disabled athlete and then grade them. In Equestrian sport there are five grades from 1A to 5. 1A being the most disabled, 5 being the least disabled. In 1996 I was graded at Grade 2, which meant the tests were ridden in walk and trot. In 2004 I was graded again as a 1A and this meant walk only tests.

The sport of Para dressage changed a lot when, in Athens 2004, the riders were selected and competed on their own horses. It changed the emphasis from solely the rider's riding ability to include how good the horse was at Dressage. Also, for grades 1 and 2, the trainers could ride the horse until the last 15 minutes before the competitor rode in the arena. This was to help prevent the more disabled people becoming too over tired to ride, or to ride the initial 'joie de vivre' out of the horse, before the disbled rider had to manage. The trainer could ride for up to an hour in any one 24-hour period. Para dressage really came to the fore after the London Games, where so many spectators came to watch.

Q. Tell me about your development as a leader in para-dressage?

A. I was always described (even as a child) as having a stubborn streak! My whole aim when I became wheelchair bound, was not to be defined by my disability. In the 80s there were no dropped kerbs, no wide doorways, minimal accessible toilets etc. I campaigned in every aspect of social care to facilitate enabling people, not limiting them by their disability and then just caring for them.

After Atlanta, there were exciting times in the development of paradressage. Before 1996 Jonquil Solt with the RDA had got 26 countries involved. After 1996, all sport was looked at very carefully. The 1996 Games was not a success for GBR especially for the able bodied. It was realised that funding was needed to enable the sports to grow and support potential sportsmen to train as professionals.

Anne and Jonquil continued to work tirelessly to fund raise for Sydney Olympics (2000) where the riders still rode borrowed horses.

By 2000 Jane Goldsmith had come into the Para scene as Coach and Lee Pearson (now Sir Lee Pearson) was evolving as a Grade 1 rider. Team gold was Anne's second Team medal for GB at Sydney that year.

RDA had 'made the sport' and started dressage competitions, but when it came to competitors receiving money to help them train, this was not a possibility. The sport had to move to protect the charitable status of the RDA which was with an emphasis on the therapeutic benefits to its riders. Lottery funding was set up which meant that competitors with proven ability to go on to win medals, could receive money from this fund to help them train full time. The sport itself was given a lottery grant to provide training, trainers and managers for the competitors. Lottery funding has contributed to the whole development of all sports. Britain has now become internationally renowned at the top of sport from 1997 onwards.

Q. Talk about riding your own horses in competition?

A. As mentioned earlier, Athens was the first Olympic Games where countries took their own horses. On one's own horse it was important for

Grade 1 riders to have a horse with an exceptional and adaptable walk. For Athens I was due to take Lambrusco, but at the last minute he was quarantined because of strangles at his yard, so I rode Odette a 15.2hh Event mare.

In Beijing I rode 'Teddy Edwards', a Welsh Cob, who had a disadvantaged back ground and was very naughty. From the first time we met we clicked, and I loved him. In Beijing we won Team Gold, Individual gold and Individual silver. That was my most special win, Teddy was naughty, but he loved being the centre of attention. After Beijing, in 2009 I was honoured with an MBE (for contribution to disabled sport) and then in 2017, after Rio 2016 I was honoured with an OBE for my contribution to para equestrian. Four consecutive Olympics, with four consecutive Team Golds was a thrilling achievement and then to receive national recognition with an MBE was an unexpected bonus, wonderfully confirmed by the 2017 OBE. An amazing honour.

Q. Which was the most challenging championship?

A. Rio 2016. I had been reserve in London, which of course at a home games was a big disappointment. By Rio I felt that I had been 'written off' as an old lady and people felt I should have retired. The Team ethos was so supportive though. One of the Dutch team had a horse named Athena that everyone loved, and we were both Grade 1A which put added pressure on me. I rode Lucas to gain two Individual Silver medals and helped win another Team Gold for GB, for the fifth time.

Q. What life lessons have you learnt from horses?

A. They have amazing empathy, they form friendships (involving the pecking order in their herd) but they form a bond with some people or riders. I certainly had that with Teddy Edwards. Horses can reason things out and are clever In the riding school some of my ponies would 'go' for some riders and be deliberately naughty for others. They are calming and can create an aura of social stability. They like to be liked and show disappointment. They taught me to be patient, consistent in my approach and to be determined to go where I wanted in life. (XRef. Pammy –Ripalong – patience. Ch.4)

Q. Who do you most admire in Equestrian Sport?

A. Pammy Hutton. She is inspirational and will never accept disability as an excuse to fail, in herself or in anyone she works with (Suzy Hext, Jonty Evans, Nicola Tustain, Debbie Criddle, Me). She inspires a 'can do' attitude and goes to the end of the line, and further, to help the people she works with. She is a great family person and this includes not only her relatives, but all who come under the 'Talland umbrella'.

Another person I admire is Nick Skelton. What a motivational man, he kept trying, overcoming a broken neck to win his Olympic Gold in Rio. I met him once and he was such an inspiring person.

Q. What do you do now that you are no longer riding as a Para dressage star?

A. I carriage drive once a week and love it. I also have time to paint and give the occasional talk on what it has been like to succeed in Horse Sport and life from a wheelchair.

Q. Do you have a favourite quote?

A. I have two: 'Do the best you can always' and 'Disability is not inability'

Reflections:
- This chapter has reminded us, and enhanced our knowledge, of some of the most exceptional equestrian sports people of our time.
- It has allowed us to indulge in the outstanding success of a range of equestrian athletes.
- It has radically confirmed the longevity of our equestrian sport. While other sports talk of veterans (Roger Federer and Rafael Nadal in tennis are 'old' for their sport in their late thirties), we are applauding our riders still competing at World class level in their fifties and sixties.
- In the next chapter we will look at some of the 'older' horses that have stayed at the 'top of their game' well into the latter part of their lives.
- Where in other sports successful athletes come and go. The longevity of our top riders conveys a familiarity with them, that those of us who love horses can continue to indulge over most of our lives.

Summary:
- Chapter Three of Eleven. We hope you are fully involved so far!
- Read on there is much more to come.
- We hope you know the riders we have already featured, research them further. Some have published autobiographies or have books of their own, detailing their skills, achievements and training methods.

Nick Skelton "Cowboy"

Nick Skelton with sons Daniel & Harry

Pammy Hutton on 'Rhyme & Reason'

Islay Auty on 'Joyett'

Jeanette Brakewell on 'Over to You' (aka 'Jack')

Anne Dunham on 'Teddy Edwards'

John Whitaker on 'Gammon'

Sir Mark Todd on 'NZB Campino'

Pammy Hutton on 'Ripalong'

Islay Auty on 'Asdic'

Jennie Loriston Clarke with 'Dutch Courage'

CHAPTER FOUR

EQUINE ICONS:

KEY POINTS:
- **Dressage**
- **Eventing**
- **Show Jumping**
- **Highlighting some special older equines.**

Here we will recognise some 'Old' horses and ponies who have achieved world class level selection and success, in spite of their age. Unique insights into some well-known equines and their winning partnerships. Here you will find some 'household names like: 'Bonfire', 'Over to You', 'Kibah Tic Toc' and 'Gammon'. There will also be some less familiar names of horses/ponies with whom the authors have been personally involved: 'Ripalong', 'Manitu N', and 'Gigolo'. While there are many instances of human athletes competing into older age, they are no longer selectable at International level in their sport – not so with the horses that we are profiling here.

RIPALONG (Eventing and Dressage at world class level in the 1970s - Pammy Hutton)

A grey part bred Arab by Rifari, he was 15.1hh (155 cm) and bought by Pammy's Mother, Molly Sivewright FBHS, for £130 which was cheap even in 1956. He was in the winning Riding Club Event team with Molly and competed in many events, hunter trials and show jumping competitions with Molly, and the head girl at Talland at that time. The whole Sivewright family shared him, winning many classes with Molly in Dressage, the Pony Club Dressage Championships with Pammy and her sister Mandy, and Windsor three-day Event three times with Pammy, who remembers the thrill of having a rosette presented to her by Her Majesty the Queen. Pammy represented GB twice at Junior European Championships in France and Germany on 'Rippy', finishing in the top twelve on both occasions. He hated water and did not have a huge amount of scope but had a big heart. She recalls that often they led substantially after Dressage, which allowed them to have one stop at whichever water Rippy disliked the most! Her younger sister rode Rippy in a Junior European Dressage team and by this time, Pammy had progressed the horse's training to Grand Prix. During this time, they also won the Combined Dressage and Show Jumping class at the Horse of the Year Show twice. (X.Ref Ch 11)

He was such a versatile horse and obviously sharing him between the family did his training no harm and working together as a family did a lot of good. When most horses are considered too old to improve, Ripalong improved. At the Horse of the Year Show in the Grand Prix, he repeated this performance at the selection trials for the Montreal Olympics 1976. Ripalong was 22 years old, surely an aged horse by anyone's reckoning, when he and Pammy were selected as travelling reserve for Montreal. Mysteriously, Rippy's passport suffered an accident where it was defaced after being dropped in a big muddy puddle, the replacement document recording Ripalong's age as 18 years old! Pammy still has the paperwork relating to that honour, it meant so much to her. Sadly 'Rippy' pulled a suspensory ligament three weeks before the Games, was unable to travel and was never truly sound again. This horse was a unique personality; he taught many a student the feel of a first flying change but could also humiliate the rider if they were over-confident or rode without tact and empathy. Pammy would say she learnt determination from Rippy, quickness and concentration but probably most of all tact. He was a horse that could not be forced, and in fact Pammy would say that sometimes she 'begged' him for his compliance.

Pammy also recollects a story of her Mother, when she was in Germany with her husband post war. She couldn't find anything to ride and eventually was lent a 21 year-old gelding with only one eye. Molly formed a bond with him, trained him with passion and the following year won the Regional Championships in Eventing on the horse. The moral of that story is, when everyone else gives up never miss an opportunity to give an old horse a chance to shine! (see ref. Gammon. Ch 4.)

BONFIRE. (Dressage – Anky Van Grunsven)

Bonfire was the Oldenburg (German) gelding owned and ridden by Anky Van Grunsven (Holland), who won four medals at World Equestrian Games and five Olympic medals. The highlight of Bonfire's career was to win an Olympic Gold Individual medal at the 2000 Sydney Olympic games when he was 17 years old. To reach this highest accolade in the closing years of his career was an outstanding feat. Considering the journey involved to the games on the opposite side of the world, plus the demands of Olympic level competition, it is again testament to the training, maintenance and resilience of this aged horse.

OVER TO YOU – 'JACK' (Eventing - Jeanette Brakewell)

This horse holds the accolade of winning the most medals for Great Britain in his eventing career. Ridden throughout his competitive career by Jeanette Brakewell, they have won four European Team Gold medals, two Olympic Team Silver medals, one World Team Bronze medal and a World Individual Silver medal. They have also finished in the top ten at Badminton horse trials five times, with seven of eight completions. He competed at his last Badminton at the age of nineteen, and retired from top level competition at the age of twenty. Jack made his only appearance at Burghley in his eighteenth year. Confounding the doubters that muttered that 'the horse was too old' to make his debut at one of the world's most challenging 5 star Events, Jack romped around the cross country inside the time (as usual) and finished in a highly credible 7th place. His final 5 star was Badminton in 2007 when he finished 14th.

Bred in 1988 in County Wexford, Ireland by Mary Lett, 'Jack' was out of a mare called 'Another Miller' by 'Over the River'. He was sold early in his life, with excellent breeding, as a Thoroughbred to fulfil a life as a Racehorse. He failed to make an impression in that discipline and after failing the vet at Doncaster Sales for a 'heart murmur' (an obscure heart irregularity) that he had throughout his life, he returned to owner Tony Clegg who at that time employed Jonty Evans,(Xref. Ch7) who spent time with the unruly 4 year-old, long reining, lungeing and handling in the 'traditional' way to gain the obedience and confidence that delivered a curious, bold horse. It was Jonty who first flagged up the innate bravery and 'joie de vivre' of the horse. Tony Clegg's daughter Fiona rode Jack briefly, but one day when attending a lesson with Chris McGrann (where Jeanette was a trainee) Jack managed to hit Fiona in the eye as she was tacking him up and Jeanette went to help her with the horse. Jack then spent some time at Chris McGrann's and Jeanette became his rider. Richard and Lindsey Marsh had decided to back Jeanette as a promising up and coming rider and they purchased Jack for her. No one had any conception of how far the partnership would go in the next fifteen years that they were together.

Jeanette speaks so emotionally and personally in her book 'Britain's Eventing Legend -Over to You' about this extraordinary horse who 'took me to places that even I never dreamt of.' Her long time Show Jumping trainer, the late Kenneth Clawson FBHS, a close friend of Islay and Pammy, was especially emotional as Jeanette and Jack climbed the leader board on the final day of the World Games in Jerez 2002. It is rare for the team pathfinder to win an individual medal. Statistically, often the Dressage on the first day of competition is seen as being less generously marked than the competitors on the second day. Many riders had faults in the Show Jumping which projected Great Britain to Team Bronze medal and Jeanette and Jack to Individual Silver.

John Bowen, Jeanette's Dressage trainer, pays a great tribute to Jeanette's management of Jack, "To retire him, sound and competitive at the age of 20 is testament to Jeanette's management and training".

KIBAH-TIC-TOC (Eventing - Matt Ryan, Australia)

Kibah Tic Toc was a thoroughbred/warmblood horse bred and owned throughout his life by Bridget (Bud) Hyem, she was the first lady to represent Australia in Equestrian in Tokyo in 1964. 'Tic Toc' was ridden to Individual and Team Gold medal wins at the Barcelona Olympics 1992, when the horse was aged 17 years. An outstanding achievement for an 'aged' horse and testament to his breeder, trainer and rider that the horse in his twilight years was winning in a world class Olympic field. The horse lived to the age of 36, and died within a couple of months of his devoted Breeder who was in her eighties.

GAMMON. (Show Jumping - John Whitaker)

This horse was German bred, owned by John's father-in-law Malcolm Barr, and won over £500,000 during his glittering career, including a plethora of International Grands Prix all over the world, Grenoble, Calgary and Arnhem to mention just three.

In the horse's 21st year his regular rider was John's daughter, Louise. A few days before the Hickstead Derby meeting John decided to give the old horse another attempt at bettering his record of second place in the class on three occasions. The horse won the class convincingly, beating John Ledingham on Kilbaha in a jump off. An outstanding result from this aged horse and a reflection of the way in which the horse had been managed throughout his life, in terms of fitness and well being to be capable of winning a world class competition at the age of 21.

MANITU N (Pony Dressage - Maria Eilberg/Lorna Edmonds/Samantha Harrison)

This pony stallion was imported to the UK by Ian Woodhead (Dressage trainer. X.Ref Ch 11) and having already had international success with a pony rider in Denmark, the pony was first ridden for GB by Maria Eilberg. (X ref Ch 2) Manitu was selected for the Pony European Dressage Team for a subsequent nine years. With Maria he won two Team Bronze, Team Silver and fourth individual, went on to win two Team Bronze and Team Silver with Lorna Edmonds and fourth individual, finally with Samantha Harrison, two Team Bronze and fourth individual. This exceptional pony was the mainstay of the British Pony Team for nearly ten years. Spending his twilight years with the Harrison family, he was a hugely talented character who gave several riders a foundation of experience and opportunity from which they were privileged to benefit.

GIGOLO (Pony Dressage - Sarah Higgins/Georgina Roberts/Kristina Rausing/Claire Gallimore/Bethany Horobin/Isobel Lickley)

This chestnut gelding was bought by Ian Woodhead as a young pony and produced in a structured way to maximise the obvious potential of this 'little horse'. Sarah Higgins, under Ian's guidance, was the first to take this inexperienced pony to European Team level at the age of just six. A Team Bronze medal in Poland was his first of a clutch of Team medals over the next twelve years. Ridden to Team medal success by Georgina Roberts, Claire Gallimore, Bethany Horobin, owned by Kristina Rausing before Claire Gallimore, and to a Team place in his twilight years by Isobel Lickley, this exceptional pony was still competing successfully at International Pony level in his twenties.

The two ponies highlighted here, demonstrate the versatility of many ponies, who tend to be more resilient and adaptable to a change of rider, than many horses. Horses tend to become specialists in their discipline under one rider, but are often less able to adapt to a change in 'pilot'.

While the horse's normal lifespan is generally in the range of 25 to 30 years, and their competitive prime years being broadly between five and late teens, this inevitably is a generalisation and depends on so many factors. These would include breeding, conformation, lifestyle, training and riding. The likelihood of all the positive factors of good conformation, temperament, trainability, soundness and a partnership developing with a competent rider, coming together at the right time with the right horse – it is probably easier to win the lottery!

Racehorses (thoroughbreds) have no outstanding records of longevity either on the flat or over fences. A horse called 'Megalala' trained throughout his career by John Bridger currently holds the record of the oldest winning racehorse in the post war period. He won a 1m 2 furlong race at Lingfield at the age of 16.

An Arab called 'Al Jabal' won the Three Horseshoes Handicap stakes of 6 furlongs at Barbury Castle, Wiltshire, aged 19.

Reflections:

- Considering the horses remembered in this chapter, the common theme running through their stories is the consistency of management in terms of gradual development, consideration of demands in training and then in competition. Frequently the consistency of owner and/or trainer/rider is a major contributing factor.
- Ponies tend to be more resilient and adaptable to changes of riders and some thrive in home after home, as long as the management and riding is of a high standard.
- The horse should always be at the centre of the consideration of what work or competition is expected of him.
- The horse has a 'joie de vivre', tenacity and resilience to be part of the 'job' he obviously loves.
- Some of these horses/ponies are still living out their retirement with their owner/riders. They have been and remain a huge part of the owner's life and eventually when the end comes, the loss is felt like losing any other member of a much loved family.
- In many instances (as with humans) if the stimulus of fitness and challenge is withdrawn from a horse, they can swiftly deteriorate into loss of muscle tone, obesity, unsoundness and other signs of old age. Many ageing horses kept well and 'in work', carry on happily into very old age.

Summary:
How privileged we are to share our existence with horses. Sometimes they take us to the most unimaginable places in our lives and those pinnacles of success or achievement are not attainable without 'the horse'.

CHAPTER FIVE

MANAGING THE OLDER HORSE

KEY POINTS:

- Veterinary developments
- Interviews with leading equine vets
- Physiotherapy
- Home care and management
- Alternative treatments

What a wealth of knowledge Islay gleaned from her conversation with Rachel Murray, World renowned Veterinarian.

Rachel graduated from Cambridge University as a Vet and then spent five years in the USA, where she became a Diplomat of the American College of Veterinary Surgeons. On returning to the UK she completed a PhD and is now recognised as one of the world's leading specialists in Equine orthopaedics.

She worked for the Animal Health Trust (AHT) for 19 years, has worked in various roles for the British Equestrian, (BEF), British Dressage, (BD), British Show jumping, (BS) and British Eventing, (BE), advised the World Class Equestrian Programme since 2009, been team Vet for countless GB teams, is an Federation Equestre Internationale, (FEI) vet and officiated as such at the London Olympics 2012.

Rachel has also trained and ridden her own horses to Grand Prix level in Dressage. She and her husband Duncan Hole (also a veterinarian) have two talented daughters following successfully in the equestrian path in Dressage and Eventing.

Q: What have been the most significant developments in the management of horses from a veterinary perspective in the last 20 years?

A: In spite of the development of diagnostic techniques such as MRI, Scintigraphy, X rays, etc, which obviously enhance the speed and efficiency of diagnosing when a horse is already 'broken', the most impact over the last twenty years is in our understanding of the risk factors that cause the damage in the first place. Understanding much more about the effect of training horses on different surfaces, saddle fitting and farriery have all moved us to better understanding of the risk of injury to the competition horse.

Q: Do you think that competition horses in the Olympic disciplines last longer these days and if so why?

A: Relating to understanding the risks, but also the breeding of horses for specific disciplines, it is now much more structured and efficient to produce the horse with the right credentials genetically to be successful in the sport for which he is destined. Breeding of horses with the 'right temperament' and good conformation to carry out the work expected of them continues to move forward greatly. In turn with good training and riding this makes them less at risk of injury.

Q: Which discipline do you think sustains horses into old age most effectively? Is that due to management or rather the particular demands of the discipline?

A: On the whole any, or all of them, but the emphasis is on good management, a good training regime that correctly develops the horses' core strength, suppleness, fitness and coordination. Variety in the training is key, with regular turn out, 'cross training' on different terrains and surfaces will all contribute to the fitness and well being of any competition horse.

Q: In your role as Vet to the World Class (Lottery funded) Programme, are you seeing older horses sustaining their levels of work more frequently?

A: The horses that are well managed, on the basis of previous points made, now carry on frequently into their late teens. (X.Ref Gammon/Over to You Ch.4) The younger generation of riders/trainers often understand more about bio mechanics of the horse, muscular development and the importance of the right nutritional balance of feeding. Feeding has also become much more specific for the needs of the older horse (or young horse) too. If horses are not over-competed, then they will have greater longevity. It is keeping horses in work for as long as possible that helps them to live longer. (X.Ref reflections Ch 5)

Q: Broadly what are the optimum years of a competition horse? Does breeding affect that answer and can the Thoroughbred Racing industry be considered in that answer?

A: So much depends on management and training, and also riding. Taking Racing first, the flat horses are 'finished' competitively by the time they are four, but they are started very young. Without generalising, the Racing industry tends to be more closed in their mindset to change. Their saddle design for example has not changed in decades. If a change of saddle made the horse run faster, they might become more open to change for improvement. The National Hunt horse would not start until it was in its sixth year, but then even if very successful it will probably only race at top level for around five years.

The horse bred for Dressage, Eventing or Show Jumping will progress more gradually but then may stay at 'the top of his game' for 8 to 10 years. A big horse may not be fully mature until he is ten and it is then important that he is not over-competed while he is still developing strength and finishing maturing. A taller long-legged horse, is also potentially at greater risk of injury, as is an older horse. The older horse must be kept in good fitness, ridden well and this may not happen if he is sold in his later years as a 'school master', and then not ridden by a high calibre rider. A top-level horse may then be downgraded to a lower level of competition, e.g. Active Walero (Dressage) produced by Nicola McGivern (European Championships Team Bronze Hickstead 2003, Olympics Athens 2004). Walero was ridden successfully at Young Rider European Championship level at the age of 20, by Susie Coleridge Smith.

As with humans, although not necessarily living any longer, the management of lifestyle has pushed back the 'geriatric' label and with good management and training, horses can continue well into what used to be considered 'old age'. A 17 or 18 year-old horse if managed well, can still compete at the top of his ability. (X Ref. 'Bonfire at Sydney Olympics (17) and Gammon at Hickstead (21) Ch 4). If the horse is dropped down one level of competition then he is easily sustainable for more fulfilling years.

Q: **What modern techniques have extended or prolonged the competitive lives of horses?**

A: Without doubt the better ridden a horse is, the longer he will last, combined with good variety of work, good farriery, good saddle fitting, cross training, variety and turn out. As the horse gets older the horse must stay well-muscled, as then the tendons will support the joints securely, the joints will be more stable and less susceptible to injury.

The risk factors to injury are common across all the disciplines. (Variable/poor surfaces; over competing; insufficient recovery time; poor tack, shoeing and riding.) There are now a wide range of commercially well structured balanced feed rations for the older horse. These are custom made to give the right nutritional balance to the ageing horse.

Q: **Is there a difference in the horse's mental wellbeing relating to his competitive work in any of the disciplines?**

A: If a horse is suffering from a low-grade level of pain (which is possibly not noticeable without professional veterinary intervention) and he is a Racehorse or Event horse, then he will probably gallop and jump with no objection. The outside stimulation of a race or a cross country course will enable him to use his adrenalin which is intrinsic in him as a 'flight animal'. This instinctive reaction will over-ride his low-grade pain and he will 'run' without showing discomfort. If, however, the horse is a Dressage horse, where he is required to carry out demanding movements needing physical effort in a relatively confined area, he may then show signs of resistance or objection when the limb or limbs are subjected to the stress which gives him the low level of pain. The horse then demonstrates action that helps him to avoid the pain he is feeling, e.g. rear, spin, plant, etc. Jumping horses can, and do, jump in very different 'styles'. Some will jump high with not great lower-leg technique, others will have excellent hind and front leg action which then can necessitate less height in the air. As long as the horse clears the fence 'technique is not judged'. Far less with the Dressage horse, who is expected to carry out the intricacies of a Grand Prix test with a 'certain picture of consistency' to the Judge for the highest marks. This means that the Dressage horse in training is likely to be required to repeat movements to aim for excellence. This can subject the horse to repetitive load injury (often high suspensory injuries). Repetitive overload coupled with many hours standing in his stable is a potential recipe for disaster with a Dressage horse. As the horse gets older his joints may also lose stability if he is not maintained in the best possible muscular suppleness and strength. Mentally and physically the Dressage horse tends to be more challenged by risk factors to his wellbeing.

Q: Do we produce our young horses better in the UK than other nations in any aspect?

A: Maybe in some instances, the young horses that are allowed to run freely as foals, yearlings, two and three year olds will do better than the youngsters that are reared in open barn systems. The knowledge base however, in countries like Denmark, where there is a well defined breeding programme for sport horses, may be far more advanced than us. The standard of farriery in the UK is probably some of the best in the world and this has a huge contributing factor on the soundness of all competition horses.

Q: Do you have a favourite quote?

A: "Everything I do is in the best interests of the horse".

John Killingbeck MRCVS

Islay enjoyed an interesting and enlightening conversation with John Killingbeck MRCVS. John with some fifty years' experience as an Equine Vet, was fascinating to listen to.

A joint Honours Degree in Zoology & Physiology and a Degree in Agriculture preceded his progression to study Veterinary Medicine. He talked about his early years spent in the David Tatlow yard, who he described as a true horseman. David's father had fought in the Battle of the Somme in the Royal Horse Artillery. David was Champion Point to Point rider five years running, before becoming a prolifically successful Producer of Show Horses. The depth of knowledge gained from the training regime, feeding and overall management of the horse was immeasurable.

When John qualified as a Vet, he was always going to follow an equestrian pathway and has covered four Olympic games, with teams from all over the world. Team Vet to the GB Senior Event Team for five years and Team Vet for Japan, Bermuda, Ireland, to mention a few of the nations with whom he has worked. He has been part of Junior/Young Rider and Senior teams for Show Jumping and Eventing, and through this aspect of his career he has assisted in the achievement of at least 20 Gold Medals at Olympic, World and European levels.

Our conversation developed from a discussion about the horse's evolution, millions of years of the world's evolution and then in some 6,000 years of the development of 'eohippus' (ref. See ch 1.) the horse is the same wild horse of centuries ago. Evolution moves incredibly slowly but human development particularly in the second half of the twentieth century has created pressures on horses that evolution cannot keep up with. The major threats to horses' longevity and soundness is the proliferation of working horses on artificial surfaces and the demands made in all areas of competitive sport.

Q: How has the management of the competition horse changed in the last 20 years, from your perspective as an equine vet?

A: Money is the biggest factor, followed by less understanding of the horse as a herbivorous, herd animal. Consider where success starts. With Lewis Hamilton (six times World Formula One Champion) it started as a small child in the garage, he would spend every waking minute understanding the mechanics of a vehicle, knowing every cog and wheel, long before he was able to drive.

With horses a rider's success is borne initially in the stable, the love of the horse, the empathy with the horse (ref. Ch 2), knowing the horse, this is the precursor to the successful rider. The spectrum of knowledge that existed in the large livery yards, hunting stables and farming backgrounds where horses were an integral part of the 'livestock' was imbued into each generation automatically. Much of that cascade of knowledge and expertise has been diluted or lost by the more intensive manner in which competition horses may be kept today. Money may purchase a talented or previously competitively successful horse but the rule book of training background is not transferred and the horse's future is dependent on the knowledge and expertise of the 'new owner'.

Q: **How can wear & tear and injury in the older horse be better managed?**

A: That is often characteristic of the background of the person that has produced the horse. Consider the way the Whitaker's produce their horses (Ref; Whitaker interview Ch 3). Horses are not machines and variety is essential whatever their specialist area of competition. Just like humans they need a good regime of feeding, weight management and structured exercise to keep mind and body flexible, strong and functioning for as long as possible.

Q: **In your opinion of owners/trainers/riders today, what do they do better and where are the weaknesses?**

A: The greatest weakness is impatience. We live in a 'quick fix' society and often with injury (even minor) the critical factor is to allow time for full recovery. Of course, a greater range of diagnostic techniques may enhance assessment of a condition but often the key is time.

Q: **What has been the most useful development in veterinary diagnostics or equipment in the last 20 years?**

A: Imaging, X-Ray, CT and MRI scans are all useful but they are expensive which inevitably limits the availability to everyone. There is a significant increase in the number of knowledgeable trainers who understand horses in a more sophisticated way. More information and time spent diagnosing a lameness will allow more shared information on how to manage it.

Q: **Have competition demands put greater emphasis on the horses' fitness and soundness, if so how or where?**

A: Fifty years ago all competition was on grass, the huge development of working horses on an artificial surface has greatly increased the incidence of lameness in the competition horse. The horses' natural ability for the muscles and ligaments to stretch and recoil on the point of impact of the foot is limited or distorted on an artificial surface.

There is an increase of social pressure and pressure from owners. More owners tend to have expectations of success, rather than just enjoy the pleasure of owning a competitive horse. Many owners used to have one horse that they recognised could go further than they could take it, but they were always interested in how the training evolved. Now there may be more owners with a need to satisfy their intrinsic gratification, which means they are more interested in the result rather than how the result was achieved. Widening the base of a triangle does not make the pinnacle any larger, the pinnacle of competition is still only achieved by painstaking attention to detail of all aspects of training and welfare.

Often horses are put under greater pressure than is appropriate for their physical age and maturity. The core strength and steady development of the young horse mentally and physically, will define his longevity and in many instances his ability to maintain good soundness. Joint problems often start to arise through a lack of balance, strength and the horse's ability to manage the power that he is born with but will take years to develop. People want an easy answer and a quick result. No Show Jumper is trained to international level by jumping bigger and more fences. The Show Jumper is trained to win by the athleticism and flexibility he develops 'on the flat between fences'.If he then has the scope to jump high and clear he can become a 'Big Star' (Nick Skelton's gold medal winning horse).

Q: What is your personal passion for horses?
A: I am constantly curious about why the horse does what he does in every situation he finds himself.

Q: Do you have a favourite quote?
A: 'Remember evolution moves very slowly'.

Emma Dainty Physiotherapist
Emma Dainty is a chartered physiotherapist who spent 15 years gaining invaluable experience in the National Health Service and working for the RAF. She then completed a Masters, in Veterinary Physiotherapy, at the Royal Veterinary College and since 2001 mostly concentrates on the treatment of horses, with some small animal 'patients' as well. She gives clinics all over the Midlands from her base in Shrewsbury and is team physiotherapist to the British Eventing Junior and Young Rider squads. Islay caught up with her during the Coronavirus 'lockdown' and gained an interesting insight into her work with horses in a variety of roles.

Q: What was your pathway into equine physiotherapy?
A: My Father spent his life in the military, and I think hoped I would follow him into the forces. I trained in human physiotherapy and worked with humans for 15 years spending a good period working in the NHS and then at RAF Cosford for 10 years, which went some way to appeasing my Father.

Q: As most of your work now is with horses, do you still treat humans and other animals?

A: Occasionally I treat humans, but I do a small animal clinic regularly treating dogs and some cats. Often people do not relate to small animals possibly needing physiotherapy as horses and humans do.

Q: In terms of treating older horses, what do you consider to be 'elderly' in a horse, or does it depend on breeding, type or what work the horse has done or is still doing?

A: I think there is a genetic link in the ageing of horses. Arabs, blood horses and native breeds tend to have greater longevity.

Q: Do horses carry on longer in competition now than 10 or 20 years ago, if so what has made the most difference to their longevity?

A: 'Yes and no'. The knowledge in the professional ranks of riders is generally more enhanced, more informed with support from farriery, saddle fitting, physiotherapy and fitness regimes. This is tempered by young horses being put under pressure early to compete in 'age' classes. This applies to all disciplines. Then there are people owning a horse for the first time in their mid life and they lack the knowledge that is established over years of 'having horses in your life'. Riding horses and many competition horses no longer have an 'off season'. Competition can be 'full on' all year which again puts horses under increased pressure.

Q: In terms of your management of the 'competition horse', does maintenance work best, or can you make similar improvement on a horse if you are called in when a problem arises?

A: It is ideal if I can know a horse prior to an injury. If I know the horse when it is 'normal', then routinely seeing the horse monthly (or even once a fortnight) it is easier to see a problem developing. Again the professional riders or riders who have been on squads before, are 'seasoned' and systematic in their routine of management.

Q: In 'modern' management what has made the most difference to diagnosis and treatment of injuries?

A: The sharing of information and expertise between veterinarians, physiotherapists, farriers and saddle fitters has all enhanced the management of the horse's well-being. Some owners can be reluctant to allow this sharing of knowledge until they accept that it is in the horse's best interest. Systems like 'Centaur Biomechanics' (ref. Russell MacKechnie Guire who has brought the latest biomechanical analysis to horses and riders at all levels) highlight rider position, straightness and effect on the horse. This can significantly help the rider to take more responsibility for their own suppleness, fitness and balance. Young veterinarians are inclined to be more acceptable to new methods of treatment.

Q: Do you have any particular 'dislikes' of management or conversely what methods of keeping horses increases their longevity?

A: Horses who are 'arena bound' e.g. they go in an arena 6 days a week and rarely hack or have little access to alternative surfaces to work on. Horses should work on a variety of surfaces and gradients, roadwork, fields, hills all for variety of interest fitness and well-being. They should be hacked in balance not allowed to 'wander along on a long rein'. Where horses 'suffer' most is at the lower levels – not through intentional neglect, but through lack of knowledge of the owner to understand the horse as a horse. A horse with one owner rider, will ultimately be affected by the strengths and of weaknesses of that rider. If the rider is crooked, unbalanced, unfit or tending to be overweight then the horse will reflect the inadequacies of his owner's shortcomings.

Q: What type or horses do you work with most?

A: I have some seasonal fluctuations, I work with quite a lot of national hunt horses from September to March and then Dressage horses, eventers, with a few showjumpers, riding club horses and 'happy hackers'.

Q: Do you have a personal favourite quote or philosophy?

A: I think I'm quite a good judge of character and I have a good sense of humour. I believe that what you see the first time you look at a horse for the first time is what you will always see. (e.g. if he has a big nose, lop ears or an ugly head that is what you will always be drawn to.)

Alternative or Complementary Treatments:
Pammy's account:

"I remember the 'wart cream' that Mother used as the 'cure all' for warts for years. Rubbed on and a few weeks later they would disappear. One day we couldn't get any more from Cornwall, so Mum had it analysed and 'bingo' it was 'Bells Udder Cream'. We also brought Gorse back from Cornwall, as that also helps with many ailments. My mother had 'healing hands', it was often not the ointment or oils that she used but the hands that were applying the treatment that caused the improvement."

Pammy rarely uses boots or bandages on any of her dressage horses, as she believes they stay sounder for longer without. A good farrier is essential in the mix of good management of the horse but Pammy would be one of a very few riders who could be riding a horse at an International show with no shoes on at all. One

such horse had been 'written off' as terminally unsound and Pammy's vet would
pull her leg each year with a cheerful, "I've come to flu vac that dead horse!"
Then there is the horse Pammy's sister owned who was ninth at Burghley even
though he had 'broken down' twice. He never had a boot or bandage on him
and never broke down again. He went round Burghley with 'Aintree plast' on,
nowadays the modern equivalent is 'Ice tight'.

As Pammy stated "Mum had 'healing hands' and treated many a person. The best I can do is positive thoughts! That is an essential key to life".

§

We have referred to the value of consistency in the care and management of horses today. We have outstanding equine veterinary specialists, then support from Physiotherapists, Chiropractors and Masseurs.

There are those who practise a range of alternative treatments: **Shiatsu** (a form of Japanese massage)
Reiki (a form of alternative medicine called 'energy healing' transferring natural healing through the transmission of energy from the practitioner's hands.)
Bowen Therapy (A holistic remedial technique that works on the soft connective tissue of the body aimed to help musculoskeletal or related neurological problems.) to mention a few.
Radionics – Holistic distant healing – is a form of complementary healing in which the practitioner 'delivers' healing 'energies' to a patient irrespective of the distance between them. A small sample of the 'patient's' hair is sent to the practitioner to reflect the 'energy' of the patient being treated. This is then used in 'the black box' (radionics machine) together with a profile of the 'patient' to help identify treatment. (X.Ref. Amanti in this chapter.)
Acupuncture – A system of complementary medicine where fine needles are inserted into the skin at specific points considered to be 'meridians' or lines of energy. It is used on humans and horses for a variety of physical (and in humans) mental conditions.

In writing this book Pammy and Islay came across a remarkable coincidence. Pammy broke her arm badly as a teenager and in her early twenties Islay suffered an ongoing problem with her neck. Following are the accounts of their individual management.

CASE STUDY:

Pammy's account:

The acute fracture of my arm when I had a fall riding resulted in a bone visibly sticking out and an emergency visit to hospital. After the routine six weeks in plaster as was the way 'back in the day', I couldn't use my left hand at all, it hung limply as if dead and I could stick pins into my thumb and fingers and feel nothing. Doctors were gloomy about the prognosis, saying I'd lost the use of it. I thought my riding career was over as did the doctors. My Mother sent me to London to see a brilliant lady – known as the 'witch doctor'. She was Mrs Raeburn, the wife of the then Governor of the Tower of London and lived in a beautiful apartment within the Tower, known as the Queen's House. She was renowned for her 'healing hands'. Without even touching me she assessed me, saying "oh yes dear and you have an injury in your left leg as well". I visited her weekly for about two months. She could generate heat and movement in my arm from close proximity to me, without actually touching me. The improvement was astounding, and I used to travel back on the train still attempting to move my fingers as she did, which for weeks I could not do, although she had made all my fingers wiggle easily when I was with her. Within six months I had my arm back fully functional, although I have always suffered some tingling in my fingers from time to time especially when I'm tired. Mrs Raeburn was having remarkable success with folk suffering from cancer and a range of other ailments and fractures. I used Mrs Raeburn again with my grand prix horse 'Amanti'. He was a very highly strung horse and tension at a competition became an enemy to my results. I sent Mrs Raeburn a small sample of hair and she put Amanti on the 'black box'. The results were astonishing, when Amanti was 'on the black box' his behaviour was always much calmer.

CASE STUDY:

Islay's account:

I was at Mrs Sturrock's yard in Rutland at the time, studying for my BHSI, working hard and riding three or four times a day. I was beginning to suffer all the time with pain down both arms into my hands and it became so bad that it woke me in the night. With pins and needles down both arms, numbness to the point that I could stick pins in both hands (and draw blood!) and couldn't feel it. My Father (orthopaedic surgeon trained, although by then specialising in Rheumatism and Arthritis) sent me to a variety of specialists who x-rayed,

81

prodded and poked, but no one had any idea what was the cause, other than there was a problem in my neck. I was fitted with a surgical collar which sorted the pain and discomfort but whenever I took the collar off the problem returned within a few minutes. Mrs Sturrock suggested I go to see the 'Witch Doctor'. My Father nearly blew a gasket, but since he had been unable to provide any relief to my problem, he reluctantly allowed me to go with the strong proviso that "she is NOT to manipulate you". I was duly ushered into the Queen's house at the Tower by a Beefeater. Mrs Raeburn stood behind me with no contact and said, "oh yes no problem, its your neck". As a sceptical 21 year old I remember thinking "I've already told you that!" What happened over the next two hours with 'the witch doctor' has stayed with me for the rest of my life. I lay full length on a couch with Mrs Raeburn kneeling on the floor next to me. She had one hand under my neck (with no pressure) and the other hand about two inches above my forehead (no contact). Then we talked about anything and everything that was topical or came into our heads. In the meantime, my body convulsed, twitched and jerked as if I had an electric current running through my length. Sometimes it would be violent (but not painful) and sometimes quite mild. Mrs Raeburn warned me each time there was going to be a strong convulsion and I asked her how she knew. "I can feel it coming through my hands" was her reply. After about two and a half hours Mrs Raeburn told me that "I was done", she told me I would feel tired for a day or two and to take it easy to allow my body to realign in its new adjustment. I asked if I would need another 'treatment' she advised hopefully not. I was indeed exhausted, felt as if I'd run a marathon, but no more pain and to this day I have not had a recurrence of that problem. It was certainly not 'faith healing' as I had no faith whatsoever that day as I travelled to London. My Father was astounded and accepted that there are avenues of 'healing' that are still to this day unexplained and unquantifiable.

§

We can all recount stories of 'healing' both of ourselves and our horses. We would always advise the orthodox methods of initial consideration of lack of well-being in either horse or rider. If or when these have been exhausted, then you may choose to seek alternative methods. Ensure that you take good advice when using alternative treatments, anecdotal evidence should come from reliable experienced sources (in our case Mrs Sivewright FBHS and Mrs Sturrock FBHS). Alternative treatments may not have the benefit of factual evidence of success, so beware of charlatans.

Maintaining the physical fitness and mental wellbeing of the horse and rider.
As modern methods evolve it is easy to forget the 'old fashioned' techniques and practices that have stood the test of time and still work. (XRef. Ch 5. Rachel Murray)

Pammy recalls one of her event horse's Gameel, he was a Gold medallist with her sister Mandy and successful with both sisters at major events of the time (Windsor and Punchestown Three Day Events). She remembers sitting on his back, standing in the river contemplating life because "he had front legs that we had to really take care of. This is a good reminder that a firm based river bed, with a gentle flow of cold water at the right depth, beats any other type of leg treatment."

The famous National Hunt racehorse Red Rum, who won three Grand Nationals, two consecutive in 1973/74, was second in 1975/76 and then won again in 1977, was trained by Ginger McCain, extensively using the firm sands of Southport Beach, Lancashire and the shallow salt water of the sea to develop his fitness. A fraction of the cost of investing in a water tread mill!

Returning to the horse that benefits from 'cross training', even if he is a specialist in one discipline, jumping the dressage horse adds quickness, variety and reaction. The dressage rider who has come to Dressage from a showing background,(e.g. Charlotte Dujardin and Louise Bell, both now International Dressage riders) will always know how to 'present themselves and their horse' for that big occasion. There are some places, in almost every dressage test and arena, that are relatively blind spots to the Judge (especially if there is only one Judge at C). This is where, with good feel and showmanship, the rider can mask a weak transition or enhance the energy for the next movement. To achieve a beautiful picture there is sometimes a need to use a touch of concealer!

This is using knowledge, timing, skill and judgement to present a beautiful harmonious picture.

Reflections:

- The availability of highly skilled specialist care for our horses in the 21st century is second to none in the U.K. and we have been privileged to share some opinions from some world class clinicians in this chapter.
- The care and management that we as lovers of horses give our equines on a daily basis can greatly assist the professional advice that we may need to seek when the horses become unwell.
- As with humans a good balance of mental and physical wellbeing for our horses is essential, to keep them in the best possible condition for whatever their age and stage of life.
- The older we get the more experience of life we have gleaned and sometimes the old fashioned remedies can 'come good' when all other options have been exhausted.

Summary:

- If in doubt then seek help. Early intervention can often be a life saver and in the long run professional advice can save money by early intervention of an unknown problem.
- Management is preferable to prevent the horse from breaking rather than remedial treatment after the horse is 'broken'.

CHAPTER SIX

MAINTAINING HEALTH AND WELL BEING

KEY POINTS:

- Mental health and wellbeing
- Identifying warning signs.
- Case studies
- Depression
- Self-help
- Sharing for support
- The role of Social Media

Much thought and consideration has been given to some of the contents of this Chapter. As a subject, it has risen to the forefront of consideration in the 21st Century. Never more so than through the Corvid 19 Pandemic that has ravaged our way of life.

The authors would stress categorically that the opinions discussed in this work, relate wholly to the broad experience of our owns lives in the horse industry and possible management of many issues relating to that personal experience, or that through our long association with the industry, we have seen.

We both feel so strongly about this subject that we have candidly shared our own individual and painful experiences of intensely personal and distressing periods of our lives, and how we came through them to better times. We are not trained health professionals and do not attempt to offer professional advice. Please avoid judging us in terms of the opinions voiced in this Chapter; rather admire us for discussing a subject that is current and more common, in the often-hectic, lifestyles that many of us lead today. If any of the examples and case studies help one person (or more) to deal with the challenges that life throws at us, then we feel this information is valuable and worth sharing. Anyone who feels we are in danger of 'touching raw nerves' please move on to another chapter.

MENTAL HEALTH and WELLBEING

In today's world we are constantly bombarded with the terms 'mental health' and 'wellbeing'. Let us take a moment to consider the definition of these terms and then the authors will try to put them into the context of our lives with horses.

(Ref: Chamber's English Dictionary)
Health = sound bodily or mental condition.
Healthy = in good health, morally or spiritually wholesome.

Depression = a sinking or lowering. Feelings of gloom, despondency and dejection.
Wellbeing = welfare.
Welfare = enjoyment of health.
Mindset = General way of thinking relating to attitudes and beliefs.
Mental = pertaining to the mind – without outward expression.
Emotion = Moving of the feelings. Agitation of the mind.
Illness = Sickness/Disease.

Identifying and understanding these fundamental terms and their meanings, opens up a huge area of consideration with regard to how a person may be thinking, feeling, and processing information. Managing the results of those thoughts and their subsequent actions will affect how a person is then able to proceed with their lifestyle. We make no apology within this book for constantly reminding the reader that within that mix of personal feelings there is the **horse**. This book is fundamentally about **horses in our lives.**

Horse = A single hoofed, herd living, herbivorous animal. A creature that thrives in a group, in the wild has a hierarchical lifestyle, is a follower rarely a leader and ultimately given the opportunity would run away and eat grass!

The horse has none of the deep thinking, reasoning power that we have, neither does he indulge in the extensive development of his emotions. His orientation is totally focused on eating, flight from 'the predator' and procreation – perhaps! Poor creature! He may then have to deal with an owner who can be emotionally charged and driven by a mindset that is totally on a different wavelength to his own.

This Chapter is going to explore some of the complexities of human mental health and wellbeing but only in the context of the authors' experience in the equestrian industry and **not** as technical health experts. If it helps bond the relationship between a person and a horse, then we have achieved success for both human and equine.

Winston Churchill was deeply involved with horses throughout his life, the following quotes are attributed to him and in our opinion are powerful reminders of what this book is about.

"There is something about the outside of a horse that is good for the inside of man."
"No hour of life is wasted that is spent in the saddle."

attributed to Winston Churchill

Please draw on these profound statements as we consider our health and wellbeing.

CASE STUDY:
Islay Auty (January 1993 to September 1994)

Islay's account:
I had worked with horses all my life, growing up in a strong family relationship with great support from family and friends, life had not really challenged me until I was in my mid-forties.
Within a period of less than two years all that changed. Starting with the death of my Father. (at 82 he had lived a fulfilled life and in the scheme of things it is predictable to lose one's parents.) Within three months a dear Aunt followed (she lived in the same village as us, came to competitions with me, took Robert to school, went to the bank for me and was truly 'my go to' for anything!) then my only sister was diagnosed with terminal cancer, my Mother had a heart attack and I was suddenly the only member of the family who was still well and functioning. Within this scenario of crises, I realised that travelling from one end of the country to the other to try to support my ailing sister (in Kent) and hospitalised mother (in Hampshire), while still being there for a teenage child, husband and sharing the running of the equestrian business (in Worcestershire), were taking a heavy toll on me physically and emotionally. Therefore, I made the life changing decision to walk away from the business I had loved, nurtured and that had been a huge part of my life for 18 years.
The death of my sister followed within months by my Mother, left me completely overwhelmed by the enormity of the losses. My hair started to fall out and within weeks I had large bald patches, from what had always been a thick and

full head of hair. Visiting my doctor and explaining my recent catalogue of losses, I was told that I was suffering 'clinical depression'.

It was described like a person swimming confidently up stream with strength and determination, gradually they begin to tire and the occasional wave washes over them, they gasp and lose some strength and efficiency, the waves become more frequent as the energy is sapped from them and eventually, unless they seek help, they succumb to the waves and go under. I completely understood that analogy.

Medication was advised, but I had always been of a strong constitution both physically and mentally, I refused. My dear Father, as a Doctor had always advocated strength of mind, self-discipline and determination to 'get over it'. In hindsight, the diagnosis of 'clinical depression' was in this situation certainly correct.

Counselling may well have helped, an independent, uninvolved, person to listen and support could probably have directed the healing process with more structure. In 'old school – stiff upper lip' way, I just immersed myself in the horses, dogs and with the support of my husband, son and a good dose of self-talk. I had suffered four huge losses in a short period of time with insufficient time to recover from one bereavement, before being confronted with a second, third and fourth.

If bereavement is an experience which needs to follow a process: numbness; anger; acceptance; recognition; of the loss and finally, appreciation of the value of the relationship, then I accumulated four emotional tragedies with no time or opportunity to manage and recover from one, before the next loss piled on top of the already existing fragile situation.

By the time four huge bereavements had occurred in relatively quick succession, my natural strength and resilience had been sapped to near extinction. In conjunction with the bereavements, I had lost my livelihood and all the familiarity, consistency and friendships that had existed in my equestrian way of life for nearly two decades. The only consistencies still in my life were my husband and son, and some close friends who 'were there when I most needed them'.

It is true, that often it takes a huge crisis in life to find out who your true friends are.

Experience is what you gain as a result of an event. That experience can then *redirect your perspective on life, it will probably influence the decisions you make, the opinions you may hold for future situations.*

My experience during those twenty months of crisis, have enhanced my awareness of the fragility of life, 'What doesn't kill you makes you stronger' certainly has applied to me and I would admit to being a calmer, more well-rounded, person as a result. I have also been able to share my own progression out of despair with others, offer support and inspiration to those experiencing their own crises. (XRef. Ch 11)

§

Mental illness is vastly beyond the remit of this book and the authors would like to state categorically any interpretation of innate or genetic mental illness, in no way overlaps with the concepts that we may touch on in terms of mental health and wellbeing of the person involved in the care, management and training of horses.

This chapter will highlight some case studies of genuine situations of equestrian workers dealing with mental health and wellbeing issues. It will also cover the generalities of managing: fitness, physical well being, nutrition and sleep within the practicalities of working full time with horses.

Working with horses is always physically and mentally demanding. Dealing with the daily demands of caring for horses includes mucking out, changing rugs, tacking up, riding, lungeing, turning out and bringing in horses, heaving weights (wheelbarrows and bales), the list is endless. Into that, add the

vagaries of the British weather, from freezing and soaked in Winter, to heat and humidity in Summer, and one has the challenge of no two days ever being the same or predictable. This has to be one of the delights of working with horses, but it can also be one of the biggest drains on one's energy, resilience and mental tenacity.

Young people going into a full-time career with horses are often vulnerable to the pitfalls of managing themselves, and their wellbeing, independently without family help. Long hours, physically demanding work and living away from home for the first time, can easily create overload mentally and physically, in a short period of time. They may have had horses at home all their lives, 'done' horses before and after school, and 'lived' horses in every school holiday. The first experience of working with horses as a full-time career option, can be extremely challenging, create fatigue, self-reliance and self-questioning that the young person has never experienced before. If a young person is living away from home where all the familiar 'home comforts' and support of Mum and Dad are cut off, the whole experience can change from a 'rose coloured dream come true' to an ongoing nightmare. If they are abroad it is even worse, if there is a language barrier to manage as well.

Depression:
Defined as: Feelings of severe despondency and dejection.

From experience, broadly speaking people fall into two categories 'cup half full people' and 'cup half empty people', or as one wise lady used to put it 'two people look out of a prison cell window, one sees muck and the other sees stars'.

From that starting point one's whole attitude on life can go in very different directions. In conjunction with that, the way those around us deal with a fundamental mindset, can hugely influence how we develop. The challenges that life throws at us can cause us to 'sink or swim'. That is categorising depression as a state of mind and using its definition rather generally.

The opinion of whether you are a positive or negative personality has been well researched and there is a general consideration that it is innate in a person's makeup. Circumstances however can endorse or reduce that inherent tendency. Environment and the interaction with others can also have a profound effect on how a personality might view or deal with the problems that life throws at us. It is easy to be 'brought down' by constantly being surrounded or influenced by negativity. An accumulation of bad circumstances, which none of us are immune to in life, can cause a build-up of negative thoughts and emotions that overwhelm even the strongest personality.

'It's not fair' is an age old, childhood, statement. As we develop, we know only too well that life is definitely 'not fair'.

Recognising that gradual accumulation of despair either in oneself, or as importantly, in a friend or work colleague, is essential in the ability to help. Otherwise the overwhelming emotions maybe take an irreversible toll on the individual.

Depression for some is an innate condition, a disease, an illness, which can be helped through medication and professional counselling. If 'depression' is persisting, then ensure that professional medical support is sought as a matter of urgency.

Circumstances in an equestrian workplace that may promote 'depression':

- Living away from home for the first time (having to cope with lack of 'home comforts', managing oneself to maintain health, washing, cooking etc.)
- Long hours with demanding physical work, often in challenging weather conditions and frequently working alone.
- Lack of clear structure of work or leadership with inconsistent management of staff, and often frequent staff changes.
- Too many horses to care for, with time off and appropriate holidays not clearly adhered to.
- Clarity of job description, variable and random change of task or responsibility expected, without regular relevant training for the work expected.
- Inconsistency in workload, often due to absence of co-workers due to illness or unexpected unscheduled absenteeism. This immediately increases the amount of work that needs to be covered by those still in attendance. (X rf. Ch 9)
- Promises of training or competition opportunities often not fulfilled.
- Poor living conditions preventing you from being warm, comfortable, clean and having peer group company, especially during minimal leisure time.
- Poor provision of balanced, regular meals and breaks appropriate to the intensity of work schedule.
- Inadequate or inconsistent training and mentoring.
- Low application of incentives and often, minimum wage barely adhered to with, 'overtime' assumed and not recognised or rewarded.
- Circumstances not living up to the expectation of the person.

We have all 'worked for the love of the horse', we are all in this industry 'for the love of the horse.' We write this book to try to identify the passion we have for 'the love of the horse', but we also identify increasingly, that just as the welfare of the horse is vital in every situation, so is the welfare of anyone working with horses of paramount importance. If a student or employee is becoming overwhelmed by their circumstances, then we have a moral responsibility to help them and to create an 'early warning system' to recognise the potential signs of the onset of 'depression' and 'not coping'.

Supporting to minimise and prevent depression in the workplace.

- Notice if someone is 'not themselves'. Know how to ask the right questions to open the opportunity to help.
- Managing a caring environment where everyone in employment has a recognised job description and regulated hours with appropriate, valued and maintained training, remuneration and time off.
- Ensuring that every trainee/employee has a 'buddy' who will support and befriend plus a senior member of the establishment to whom they feel they can turn and confidentially share worries. This senior member of the establishment must not be the best friend or partner of the 'boss', for obvious reasons.
- Regular (weekly) meetings of staff and management to review progress and discuss any issues.
- Awareness of each member of staff to recognise early signs of loss of enthusiasm, time keeping, personal commitment, mixing with others, changes in riding ability, temper, sense of humour, eating habits or involvement with others.
- Ensuring that everyone 'has a friend' and no one is isolated.
- Ensuring good communication with family, partner, siblings or friends of an employee.
- Ensure good habits of work, rest, recreation, diet and fitness (especially with young people in their first situation away from home).
- Encourage openness and sharing of 'highs and lows.
- If someone wants to talk – take time to listen and listen to hear, not to ignore, judge or make excuses for their concerns.
- 'Racing Welfare' are already embracing the need to recognise that young workers in the racing industry may need support. They are running courses through 'Mental Health First Aid England' to highlight the need for awareness, to equip people with the skills to support mental health in their own workplace.
- **Please be assured that in the majority of establishments within our amazing industry, there is a strong awareness of how challenging the nature of working with horses can be. Many yards will be totally aware of the points that we have drawn attention to here and will take every measure to ensure the wellbeing of their workforce.**

CASE STUDY: PAMMY HUTTON

Pammy's account:

At the time I was developing as a successful Event rider, and Instructor. 'Happily married' with a baby daughter Francesca, then within one year my life imploded.

The year described here became the most difficult of my life. Discovering that my first husband's eyes wandered towards any young horsewoman that took his fancy, was shattering. Divorce was then pending when I suffered a bad accident while eventing (across country) and broke my back. Within that tragic year, Francesca died in an incidence of 'cot death'.

There is a family history of depression and I admit to feelings of total despair at times, even contemplating driving at speed into a motorway bridge. As with Islay, clinical depression, due to an accumulation of punishing experiences, was certainly my condition. 'Happy' pills prescribed made me feel fat and lazy, which was worse than the desperation my tragic circumstances had promoted. The pills can become a crutch, a necessity that becomes a dependency.

As with Islay, I took myself in hand 'giving myself a serious talking to', determined to turn my life around I tackled my situation one step at a time. I abandoned the pills and looked after my weight, gradual rehabilitation of my injury and a return to riding. Small steps turned into larger steps of 'rebuilding myself', surrounding myself with people who believed in me and would give me positive support was vital in terms of my ability to 'rebuild my life and my own mental state'.

§

Taking both case studies which are genuine, true, but historical by many decades, life continues to throw such horrors at everyone at some time in their life. Often, and inexplicably, the tragedies come in multiples, which make the management of them more intense and vital to deal with.

We tend to live in a more sanitised world now, where every situation is analysed and identified in fine detail. This may have given many options and opportunities for dealing with them, but has also reduced the immediacy of taking responsibility, and giving ourselves a 'kick up the backside'. In effect are we losing the ability to 'pull ourselves together' and 'maximise our sense of survival?

Self-help:
- Professional medical advice should be a priority, if appropriate.
- Of course, seek sympathy and support which should be forthcoming from trusted family, friends or a mentor who knows you well.
- Surround yourself with 'positive people', avoid the 'doom merchants' who will share your wallowing in the depths of despondency.
- **Share** your worries and emotions. Allow someone to listen and support.
- Work out what you **need** to do and what you **want** to do to change the situation.
- You get out of life what you put in and usually that involves hard work.
- Discipline is sometimes a neglected word in our sanitised 'snowflake' world but there is limited achievement without hard work and self discipline.
- Hard work can then deploy your negative thoughts and emotions and begin to put you back on the path to 'self-worth'.
- If you sit feeling sorry for yourself and give up, this is taking the easy option, but then beware of taking out your personal feelings of failure on others.
- One small step today can start to bring about change. **You** have to make that choice to make the first step – it's your choice and puts you in control.
- This is where a 'mentor' can support and help you find the right stepping stones to make those mini steps towards a positive change. Often this can be just an older person or a friend, who has been in the same situation themselves, moved through their personal catastrophe and can identify with what you are experiencing and offer immeasurable help.
- Try to adopt a consistent daily regime of good eating and sleep.
- Show some self-discipline and order.
- Be brave and fight for yourself.
- If you sit around 'making it someone else's fault' then you can only expect to feel worse, that is your choice.
- Use messages of inspiration to help self improvement and take one day at a time.

- There will still be bad days but try not to punish yourself if you have a 'bad day'. As with any change of anything it takes time to establish and secure the new regime.
- Congratulate yourself regularly on the 'good days' and walk on from the bad days, gradually they will become less frequent and less influential.
- Remember that the horse does not understand your depression, he has no knowledge of your sadness, but he deserves to have the positive you back.
- When despair overwhelms you, go out to the stables and sit with your horse, hug him, bury your nose in his neck and cry if you need to. Tack up and go riding, feel the wind in your face and the power of the horse beneath you. Gain strength and solace from your partnership with him, horses are great healers.

- If nothing else on a 'bad day' talk to someone you trust and don't give up.
- **You** are valuable, you must fight for yourself.
- Building personal resilience is as much an art or skill as learning to ride or train a horse better.
- **Discipline, Determination**, **Drive** and **Dedication** can be four of the most powerful words for a 'life with horses'.
- Those words can be your foundations in good or sad times
- Taken in isolation they can be useful, to put small stepping stones in place to move you further away from despair, and towards positive feelings and achievement.
- Taken as four brave cornerstones of your life, they can build a resilience which will serve you well through life.
- Those words will give your life structure and decision making that the horse will clearly understand.

Consider the 'Serenity Prayer':

**"God grant me the Serenity to accept the things I cannot change,
The Courage to change the things I can and the
Wisdom to know the difference".**

(originally published in 1951 – Author: Reinhold Niebuhr)

Sharing:
Opening up about one's state of mind is often the most difficult thing to do.

The perception that a depressed person is a weak individual is a complete fallacy. Depression is not a sign of weakness. It is often a sign of trying to stay strong for far too long before seeking help. Individuals are often incredibly strong, and they continually punish themselves for having despondency, hiding it because they blame themselves for their personal lack of management and strength. Often it may be a denial from the person suffering from the increased load that depression conveys on them. One of the most valuable steps towards managing depression is to share feelings with a close friend or relative. Sharing brings in support from another source, which may positively see the problem from a different perspective and be able to offer sympathy, support and share a plan for development out of the despair.

Sharing will also ensure that if the condition is too severe to be managed in a non-professional environment, the support can develop into advice from trained practitioners.

Social Media:
'Children of the 1950s and 1960s knew nothing of today's technological age. There was nevertheless an explosion of development during those years following the austerity of the second world war. Regeneration, not only of building, employment and family life but socially, as travel expanded in all forms and the generation felt liberated and free.

'Flower power', liberal free thinking and an 'anything goes' culture evolved. There were gremlins in that 'idyllic' period. Young people could fall foul of 'Speed' (amphetamines which gave the taker a frenetic 'high'), LSD (a drug that caused hallucinations that could generate behaviour where the taker could feel they could 'rule the world' by flying off the top of a building!). Oh yes, the 50s and 60s had their own share of pitfalls and temptations that could snare the carefree and cause their downfall. Old values were eroded and a 'love for all and with all' attitude developed. This freedom needed understanding and managing. It caused consternation to the generation who had grown up through the war years, where the only priorities were to stay alive and to save the country from invasion.

The explosion of technology since the 1980s has similarly overwhelmed today's generation and has plunged many youngsters into a roller coaster of managing, not only normal emotional development through teenage years, adolescence to adulthood, but a maelstrom of media sites that demand perfection and achievement as the key to success in life.

In addition to Facebook, Instagram, Snapchat & Twitter, to name but a few media platforms. The onslaught of 'no holds barred' and 'leaving nothing to the imagination' on television regarding, murder, war, childbirth and relationships, means that youngsters grow up so much faster than in previous decades. Innocence is rare these days and that only serves to overload the young person about decisions of choice, decisions that in the past were often delayed until the young mind understood more about themselves and life in general.

We cannot protect youngsters from the generation into which they have been born, but we can help support them and balance the intensity of the technological influence, with constant awareness of maintaining secure parameters of behaviour. Just as a horse needs consistent training through clear, understandable boundaries, so do developing youth. Secure parameters show caring and commitment to that young person's wellbeing. The parameters may be 'kicked against' but nevertheless give the person a feeling of security and support, so that they can develop their own self-discipline and awareness of good and bad decision-making. Ultimately, as a parent, you must trust and hope that the training and parameters that have been put in place for your young person, will act as a safety net when they need to make choices in your absence, or may be challenged by a path that could lead them into a bad place or harm, if their choice is deflected. Developing a personality where you stays true to the values and beliefs that are instilled in you as a child give an invisible 'armour' to help maintain safety in adversity, and within life's journey.

A well trained horse will always be manageable in unforeseen circumstances, as he reverts to his basic training of obedience and submission to the leadership of the rider. A horse that has had bad or abusive training at some stage in its life, will revert to the fight or flight instinct when feeling threatened.

REFLECTIONS:
- Mental health is as important as physical health; it applies to our horses as well as us.
- Look after yourself with the same attention that you care for your horse(s)
- Good structured lifestyle regime. Sleep, nutrition, work/recreation balance, good support of family and friends.
- Development of good physical fitness needs consideration. The active work of being involved with the care of horses ensures a gradual development of physical fitness. The need to maintain physical wellbeing through the management of flexibility, cardiovascular fitness, weight control, regular good eating and sleep habits will consolidate physical wellbeing.
- Surround yourself with positive support, close friend(s), valued mentor, to assist in progression in your career and life choices.
- Social Media can be a double-edged sword. Enjoy the positive aspects of it, the camaraderie, friendship, humour and sharing. Be aware of the darker side of 'addiction to social media'.
- Share the ups and downs of life with close and trusted family and friends.
- Talk to a trusted friend and use messages of inspiration for self help.
- There is always a way through even the darkest times, the key is finding the right source of support and help.
- 'Life' is hard work, but hugely rewarding. Everyone on this planet experiences the highs and lows of life, the achievements and disappointments. Dealing with the variations is what gives us resilience and appreciation.

SUMMARY:
- Depression is a growing epidemic and one has to consider where some of the 'get up and get on with it' cures have gone, alongside some excellent progressive modern techniques to help the deeper seated problems.
- However annoying you might find this statement, 'there **is** always someone worse off than you are'.
- This does not mean that your despair at a specific moment is not the most important issue for **YOU** at the time – of course it is.
- Ensure that someone you trust, you can talk to and they will take the time to listen, is there for you.
- If you can't find that 'someone' or they are not immediately available, until you can and you <u>must</u>, then find a horse - your horse - any horse, will be completely non judgemental of your state of mind - your horse - any

horse, will patiently 'listen' to you and enjoy your company.
- There really is nothing on this planet – if you love horses – that is any substitute for time spent with a horse when you are 'feeling low'.

CHAPTER SEVEN

FITNESS TO RIDE:

KEY POINTS:

- The rider the athlete
- Coming back to riding after a break (children/work/finances/injury)
- Unique interviews - Suzannah

Hext, Jonty Evans.
- Case Studies - Bob Champion.
- Starting riding later in life
- Maintaining fitness to ride
- Veronika Mills (Equi-pilates)

Riding at any level is a sport, this by necessity requires a degree of physical fitness from the horse (mentioned in other parts of this book) and certainly from the rider (depending on the level of riding and/or competition). We have discussed empathy and feel, (see Ch.2) and that empathy is greatly

enhanced by the physical and mental state of the rider. All of us who educate riders have a shared responsibility to encourage them to be aware of the physical and mental attributes they should work to develop, that will enhance their ability to be more in tune with the horse. This can only enhance their role as an athlete plus, their effectiveness and coordination with any horse.

If fitness can be fundamental in the wellbeing and development of a child, then foundations of good health are more likely to be established for a lifetime.

With the increase of our sedentary lifestyle, more application to 'screen time' rather than outdoor play time is predominant. More children being driven to school rather than walking or cycling, coupled with the availability and acceptance of 'junk food and sweet drinks' as the 'norm', means we are seeing an evolving generation of young people with a tendency to be indolent, inactive and overweight.

Any sport requires a disciplined approach to training and fitness. Particularly any equestrian sport, will suffer from 'athletes' who are unfit, unfocused and then tend to blame their partner 'the horse' for their lack of ability and/or success.

We are doing any rider, but especially our young people, a favour if we can encourage them to take their commitment to riding horses with the same seriousness that a swimmer, gymnast, runner or footballer would apply.

Riding requires, coordination, suppleness, cardiovascular fitness, stamina, muscular tone and flexibility, hand to eye coordination, core stability and a calm focused thought process.

A degree of confidence is also an asset. Horses are aware of riders who have an underlying fear of what they are doing. The relationship with a horse is based on the rider 'being the leader,' even with a novice rider. Fear of the actual activity may inhibit that relationship and limit the development of empathy between horse and rider.

All the above attributes are easier to achieve and maintain if laid down in childhood or adolescence, although riding is not necessarily seen as an 'early development' sport. There are many instances of riders taking up the activity much later in life and then developing 'as high as they want to go'.

While early opportunity in anything tends to convey an easier habitual competence, there is a big **HOWEVER** coming up here. Anyone can achieve anything they put their mind to under most circumstances, even if they have not had an early life opportunity to pursue that dream.

Returning to riding after a break:
Depending on the reason for the interruption and assuming that the person had ridden to a basic level (or higher) of competence before the break, let's consider the pros and cons.

Pros:
- Past experience conveys a basic understanding of the sport and some awareness of the task ahead.

- If the time out was due to family commitments or financial constraints and those circumstances have now altered for time and resources to be allowed back into the picture, the only barrier will be developing skill and consistency again.
- The drive or passion to want/need to be able to ride again is overwhelming. (X Ref. Suzi/Jonty case studies)

Cons:
- If the time out was due to injury, then there may be confidence barriers that need to be overcome, and possible remedial rehabilitation incorporated into the reintroduction of the riding. (X.Ref: Suzi Hext/Jonty Evans)
- Cooperation from a rehabilitation support 'team' for the injured rider is essential. 'Buy in' from parents, friends, physios etc. will help the coordinated focus of the rider. (This is evident from the case studies highlighted.)
- Sensitivity and/or the right pressure at the right time in the role of the coach liaising carefully with the rider is essential. (ref: Jonty Evans rehab to ride)

Interview: Suzannah Hext
Islay spent a fascinating and uplifting conversation on the telephone (during lockdown for the Corvid 19 crisis) with Suzannah Hext, about her life with horses.

In 2012 when Suzi was 23 years old, she suffered a life changing accident with a young horse she was training, when the horse came over on top of her, crushing her under half a ton or more of weight. She was airlifted as a major emergency to the Radcliffe Hospital in Oxford, where she spent the next 170 days and underwent 9 operations. Her pelvis was badly shattered with major injury to her back and legs.

Q: Tell me what you remember about the accident?
A: I was riding a young horse at home near Fairford, Glos, it was a few days before the London Olympics. We had tickets for the Eventing, which I was looking forward to. At that time, I was competing my experienced horse at 3 star level (now 4 star), I was building up my profile and work independently, while working part time as a Veterinary Nurse. As I am small enough to ride ponies, I was focusing on being able to bring on young ponies for Eventing as an income source, and enjoying developing my experience, having been previously long listed at Young Rider level

(U21) for Europeans. It was a freak accident, but it changed my life forever in that instant.

Q: Can you describe your feelings as the awareness of your injuries and the consequences impacted on you?

A: Immediately, as I lay on the ground and was drifting in and out of consciousness, I knew that I couldn't feel my legs and I knew what that meant. I kept saying to the paramedics who were treating me that I couldn't feel below my waist. It was particularly hard for my parents as I had already had a bad accident from a horse when I was 13, when I broke my pelvis.

Q: What were you told in the early months following your accident?

A: I was in the John Ratcliffe Hospital in Oxford for four months, then in and out of hospital for the next two years for various operations and treatment. I was frequently told that I would never ride again, and often enough that I would probably never walk again. I never believed that. There was one Neuro Surgeon who treated me and he was the only one who shared the belief that I would and could ride again. While I was in hospital the Olympics came and went, of course we couldn't go. Then I started to watch the Paralympics which motivated and inspired me. I was having physiotherapy with an amazing lady called Gemma and she suggested I bring my saddle in for my physiotherapy sessions. It gave me a real kick to go into hospital in my wheelchair, with my saddle on my lap – it did make people stare! Gemma further encouraged me with work on my saddle.

Q: What or who started you riding again?

A: I had trained with Pammy Hutton since I was a child and she told me to get in touch with RDA in Cornwall (where we were living). That's what I did, and I rode a dear horse called 'Buster at the Camelford RDA group (it was covered by BBC South West). I rode again for the first time in two years and I could not stop smiling. Even though my pelvis had been shattered, I had a screw in my back and a battery pack in my spine, the moment I rode I knew I'd got my life back. It somehow gave me back my identity and direction. For two years I had felt that I had lost my sense of identity, I didn't know who I was anymore and certainly didn't know where I was going. My family and friends got me through those darkest days.

Q: Describe the progression of your development to Paralympic competition and world class selection?

A: Once I had ridden at RDA, I went back to Talland and I first rode Pammy's 'Amo'. Such a fabulous mare, who gave me back a sense of purpose and I competed her a bit in able-bodied Dressage classes. Then Pammy insisted that I get myself 'classified' as disabled, which I did and was graded 3. In 2015 I started riding 'Abira'. This amazing horse has competed internationally in Young Rider Teams with Charlie Hutton and is trained to Grand Prix. I 'clicked' with him the first time I rode him. By January 2016 I had been recognised and accepted onto the World Class lottery funded potential programme for Para riders. From there I continued to progress and was shortlisted for Europeans for 2017. The Championships were held in Gothenburg, Sweden. Abira and I contributed to the Team Gold medal and then claimed Individual and Freestyle Gold in Grade 3.

Q: Which medal or achievement has been the most special?

A: On the last day of Europeans (Freestyle) I was struggling with fatigue, mentally and physically as it had been a very draining week. Emotionally, obviously we'd had some amazing 'highs' but it had also taken its toll on my body and I was exhausted. As I went down the centre line in the Freestyle, it was as if Abira knew he had to 'carry me'. All I can say is that he 'did that test for me' and it was the most special experience. I just love that horse so much. He 'knew' he had to help me, and he did. That was an experience of a lifetime.

Q: What has been your biggest disappointment since your accident?

A: Obviously the accident itself changed my life. Everything I was gradually building up to was suddenly taken away from me. The hardest thing has been dealing with the increased disability. Not having the body I used to have, but still expecting more of my body than it can give. The biggest disappointment though was recently, when I was re-graded from 3 to 2 and had to accept that my disability was increasing. I felt immense disappointment over that. However, it was put into perspective and helped my acceptance of it, when I was named reserve rider for the Para dressage Team for the World Games in Trion, USA in 2018.

Q: Who or what has been your greatest motivator in life (before or since your accident?)

A: I am very self motivated especially by seeing or feeling improvement. I drive myself hard. I want to make my family, Pammy and other supporters proud of me. My parents, family, friends and Pammy have been my greatest supporters.

Q: What are your future goals?

A: I was using swimming as physiotherapy, and to improve my fitness and suppleness to ride. Then my swimming Coach suggested that I could get classified for Para swimming. The grading is slightly different to equestrian, there are 10 grades for physical disability in Swimming and I am graded 5. For 2020 I was aiming for Olympic selection in swimming and had already gained two medals in my grade at the end of 2019 in the World Para swimming games. Swimming would have a narrower window of opportunity according to my age than equestrian, and as I no longer have a top horse, that was my focus towards Tokyo 2020. I swim 50m, 100m and 200m Freestyle. Both while swimming and riding, I am able to forget my disability and I feel free, but that feeling is at its best on a horse.

Q: What do 'Horses for Life' mean to you personally?

A: Trust, friendship, partnership, empathy. When I'm in the saddle I forget the challenges. It is when I feel most free and in harmony with the horse. Horses are therapy, when I feel down, I go and see my old event horse in the field. She is 28 now and was my Young Rider horse. She's amazing, although she is only 15hh she's so strong, she's stocky and loved her jumping. She always did a good Dressage but struggled a bit to make the time, although she was brave as a lion and would jump anything. She doesn't look or act her age and I can always find peace and comfort just being with her.

Q; Describe yourself in three words:

A: STUBBORN, then Suzi asked Islay 'oh maybe that's not good?' Islay said on the contrary that's what makes you so tenacious I suspect, and it was one of the traits Anne Dunham attributed to herself too. (XRef. Jonty Evans & Anne Dunham interviews)
RESILIENT.
MOTIVATED.

Q: Favourite quotes?

A: "The things we can't change end up changing us".
"If it doesn't challenge you, it doesn't change you".

§

Telephone interview with Jonty Evans.
Jonty Evans - The Irish Olympic event rider who's horrific fall at Tattersalls International event in June 2018 captured the event world's sympathy, as he

battled through over fifty days in a coma, granted Islay a fascinating telephone interview. The following dialogue gives an insight into the tenacity and sheer determination, not only to survive, but to re establish the partnership that he has with Cooley Rorke's Drift better known as 'Art'. The story of Jonty's success with 'Art' to take him to ninth individual place at the Rio (2016) Olympics, followed by the amazing response to a crowd funding mission to secure the ride for Jonty, when the horse was offered for sale after Rio, may well become a future story in it's own right. (watch this space for a future Jonty Evans Biography)

Q: At what stage did you begin to realise how injured you were?

A: "It was seven and a half weeks that I was in a coma in hospital in Dublin. As I started to emerge from the coma, my Mother was the first to notice the differences, in fact she and my sister (Hannah) disagreed, Hannah was not convinced but my Mother insisted that I was 'coming round'. It was not like 'flicking a switch' and I woke up. For me it was a hazy development of awareness of things going on. In fact the memory of that time tended to come and go and now I can remember little of it clearly. One moment of clarity I do remember and that was one day I was awake and thought clearly 'oh that's fine, I'll ride tomorrow', then I realised my legs didn't work. I would say that I have not forgotten anything long term but my short term memory is much more compromised."

Q: Talk through the initial stages of your recovery.

A: "There is no time scale, sometimes you're feeling 'good' – thinking you're making progress – but that is open to interpretation. The medics tell you how bad it is – in a kind way, but saying it how it is. You begin to realise the severity of it all and your mind runs away with you."

"They got me up quickly but I had to go everywhere in a wheel chair, to the bathroom, to the physio, to go back to bed and sometimes I had to wait (often a long time) to be helped back into bed, it was times like that that I started to feel frustrated and tried to get myself up – then I realised I couldn't stand up."

"The medics were clear and very realistic, they weren't downbeat but they were negative about me walking. They kept referring to a 'significant brain injury'. It is difficult to remain positive in these circumstances, but I have a huge innate ability to think positively – I don't have to **try** to be positive, I just **am** extremely determined and positive." (X.Ref:Ch 6)

Q: Was there ever a time when you felt you might not be able to ride again?

A: "No absolutely not, that was never an option."

"By this time I was in Phoenix Park, Dublin beginning a period of recuperation, my Mother, sister and a friend Mike, would take me for walks (in my wheelchair) in the grounds and it was there that I made my first attempt to stand up – and couldn't."

"I was frequently told that my period of recovery was between 12 and 24 months and then that 'window of opportunity' was closing."

It made me realise what a huge effort and focus both William (Fox Pitt) and Laura (Collett) must have put into their recovery and return to successful competition after their eventing accidents."

"From the Phoenix I was moved to the Walton Centre, Liverpool, The Sidney Watkins building for the rehabilitation of patients with Brain injuries, then on to the Oaksey House rehabilitation centre in Lambourn run by the Injured Jockey's Fund. Oaksey House treats riders who are completely self-driven to recover from however severely they have been injured. That approach suited my determination to ride again, not if, but when.

Q: Who or what was your greatest motivator during your recuperation?

A: "Art has been the absolute constant – and there are few in life. He puts up with everything. I always knew he was special and a great competition horse but what he has done for me now outstrips anything he has done as a competition horse. If there was an 'equestrian equivalent' he should be 'Sir Art'. I am not sure who's quote it is but I use it about Art" – **'You fell but I've got you'.**

Q: After your injury, how long was it before you saw Art again and how did that feel?

A: "It was the weekend of Osberton (October 24th) I went to Andrew Downes yard where he had been since my accident.) Stuart Buntine (Bede events) had been fund raising for me at Osberton which made me realise how amazing was the support and strength of feeling I was receiving from the eventing 'family'. It was truly humbling. My parents and Jo Lees (friend) were with me. I felt emotional and elated when I saw Art, the same feeling I had when we achieved the crowd funding total to keep Art."

Q: Who was pivotal in getting you back on a horse and how did it feel the first time?

A: Jane Felton who used to work for me had a friend called Philippa, she had a horse called 'July' who was wide, short and secure he'd done RDA work.

As soon as I was on, I felt at home again – that was where I was meant to be – I rode July for a couple of weeks and then I wanted to go faster! So then I got on Art – he just knew I wasn't how I used to be, he looked after me, hence the quote – **'you fell but I've got you'**.

Q: Talk through the stages of progress in your riding and what gave you the greatest satisfaction?

A: "I started going to Talland and working with Pammy and Brian. Pammy encouraged my stubbornness. Brian started me jumping again and one day soon after I started jumping (I may not have told Pammy!) I fell off – Brian and I were both very satisfied as 'it had to happen sooner or later' and it made no difference to my progress in fact it probably got rid of an invisible hurdle.

Q: Talk about the relationship with Art and what has changed you in this whole experience.

A: "Everything I do now I have to think about how to do it. I'm left handed but my right side is more affected and so I deliberately do things with my right hand as I want to be better, I use my right hand more. E.g. there are two steps down into the tackroom and I concentrate on leading with my right foot each time I go down those steps.

I have always pushed myself, now I have to be careful, now I have to learn 'how to push' 'how/when and in what direction' I will move up the grades again but little by little. I have learnt to 'see myself', I will be more aware of people's feelings. People call me an inspiration – I don't see that in myself, I'm stubborn as hell and will never give up and if others see that as inspiring then I am glad."

Q: Describe yourself in three words?

A: STUBBORN AS HELL!

§

Both authors have experienced back injuries during their lives, not an unusual occurrence with riders, given the stresses and strains that work in the equestrian industry conveys on the individual's back. Falling off horses, pushing wheelbarrows and heaving weights all contribute to the potential injuries that those involved with horses may encounter.

Pammy suffered a broken back, and Islay went through surgery for a severely prolapsed disc. (X.Ref Ch7 & 11) In both cases a period of rehabilitation was essential and then a lifelong regime of stretching before riding and maintaining a structured regime of weight control and fitness to minimise further injury.

As one gets older, sitting in sitting trot can be tricky, also rising trot on increasingly arthritic knees. When pregnant or older, walk or canter are the easiest paces to sit to. With a big moving or stiff horse, canter can often be the gateway to an easier trot afterwards.

Pammy was taught that some 'in Germany' taught all the movements in canter first and then moved to trot. She can't recall who said that!

Certainly improving the balance is often easier in canter and in most cases the trot improves after.

With some of today's young they spend many more minutes in trot each and every day in their quest for perfection. Horses don't know about perfection, so the rider has the potential for constant disappointment for not reaching that goal. More brief rests for horse and rider, maybe for different reasons, with a variety of work have been highlighted by many who have contributed to this book.

Time off to give birth may convey other barriers. If the expectant mother continued to ride well into the pregnancy, then usually the return is much swifter than if riding was abandoned as soon as pregnancy was confirmed. Pammy and Islay both rode throughout pregnancy and returned to riding within days of giving birth. Islay's doctor Father told her, it was what she did every day so why stop, she just avoided riding horses she didn't trust. Generally speaking, ladies involved as professional riders/coaches who ride daily, often several horses a day, will continue to do what they do every day, until the birth is only a few weeks or days away. Their return is also likely to be swift and unhindered by a loss of fitness, core strength or confidence. Amateur riders, however, may take longer to adjust and fit horses back into their lives. For the professional rider/coach it is 'going back to work'. Amateur riders may experience a loss of confidence and 'nerve', attributing this to the increased awareness of now having responsibility for another 'human being'. Compare this to all the other things that are part of life, driving, taking a train/plane or long journey so this 'fear' is rather irrational and should be put in perspective.

The returning rider may need guidance in:

- How often they can ride.
- How they plan their redeveloping fitness supported by other exercise, e.g. swimming, walking, cycling, pilates, yoga, other cardiovascular activity.
- Setting small achievable goals to motivate and maintain ongoing progress.
- Building riding and horses back into your life can take some time and will certainly take some managing with 'significant others, (e.g. partner, children, other family or friends etc.)

- Horses inevitably put a greater strain on financial resources, certainly on available time and in balancing that 'horse/non horse' equation. (x Ref: See Ch 9)
- It is considerably easier to manage that balance if another member of the family (other half/daughter/son etc) have the same passion and commitment as you do. If you are the only one then 'good luck', you will need plenty of resilience to the 'oh you're not going riding again'/'can't you give the horse a miss today?' comments. If you can enlist the support of your 'other half' to be groom/driver, coffee maker/dressage test caller/dog walker around the course, then you are well on the way to developing a lifestyle of which a horse makes a seamless entrance and becomes 'part of the family'.

CASE STUDY: Bob Champion
(Aldaniti - Winner Aintree Grand National 1981)

Bob Champion, a successful 'jump' jockey of his era, was diagnosed with testicular cancer in 1979. His personal battle to overcome this disease and fight his way back to health and fitness is well documented, in a book and a film 'Champion'. His equine partner 'Aldaniti', trained by Josh Gifford from Findon, Sussex, had also been confronted by health issues that challenged his ongoing soundness and fitness to run the reputedly, most challenging steeplechase in the world. The combined determination of Bob to regain health and fitness for his dream goal to ride Aldaniti and compete in 'The National', plus the trainer's commitment to get a horse that had been all but written off, fit enough to run for his life in the National, are what many would call a miracle.

In April 1981 this miracle occurred. Bob Champion and Aldaniti won The Grand National to the rapturous delight of a full crowd at Aintree and the adulation of millions who watched the race on television worldwide. This led to the establishment of this partnership as legends in Equestrian Sport. Bob went on to be awarded an MBE in 1982 and in 1983 the Bob Champion Trust was founded, which has proceeded to raise millions of pounds for cancer research. (info@bobchampion.org.uk)

STARTING RIDING IN LATER LIFE:
Many of us have enduring 'dreams' – 'oh I'd love to be able to play a musical instrument' or 'I'd love to learn to ski'. Many people yearn to be able to ride a horse but have never had the opportunity. Lack of time, money, other individual circumstances and support have eluded them and then the opportunity arises, and it is time to 'seize the day' 'carpe diem'.

How to get started:
Find a riding school (preferably British Horse Society (BHS) Approved, to ensure good standards of instruction, horse care and welfare.)or if not BHS approved then by recommendation.

Go as a visitor (perhaps not indicating your intent to become a rider) to find out whether you are made to feel welcome, the establishment is tidy and has an air of good management and organisation. A member of staff gives you time and is interested in your interest in the centre.

Take a supportive friend with you and if you like what you see then broach the subject of your desire to take some riding lessons.

Always be honest about your own feelings and avoid giving any false impressions. If you are nervous, then say so. If you suffer from any aches and pains, old injuries or current conditions such as asthma, diabetes, allergies then ensure these are understood and noted on your profile.

A well-run riding school should be keen to get as much information from you as they can, as this will ensure they can maximise your needs, while not making any assumptions about what you can or cannot do. Name, address, date of birth, height, weight, and person to contact in case of emergency, would be fundamental information to have on file for any rider. Any previous experience would also be noted, although this would not be relevant to a new rider. The reason for choosing to learn to ride later in life may be of interest and relevant.

It is never too late to start, so do not be dissuaded by 'friends' who tell you that you are 'too old'. In the 21st Century we are never too old to do anything!

The day after your first riding lesson, you will discover that there are muscles that you did not know you had, and these have been tasked to support and balance you as you took your first ride!

Don't be put off, take a hot bath, relax, stretch and wait a few days until the discomfort wears off. Be aware of the muscles that are 'shouting at you' and use some stretching, swimming or Pilates to encourage those muscles to adapt.

Before you know it, and with regular riding (minimum of once a week), you will be enjoying all the benefits that learning with this wonderful creature can offer you.

Maintaining fitness to ride:
Two well used statements ring true: 'If you want something done then ask a busy person' and 'if you don't use it, lose it'.

Anyone who has any regular involvement with horses will know that 'we are always busy'. Horses are greatly dependent on the relationship with us humans, to co-exist with health, fitness and well-being.

In the frenetic era in which we now live, we are often told to relax more, slow down and avoid subjecting ourselves to 'stress'. (X ref. Ch.8????) Stress is regarded as harmful to us, but this is only the case if the 'stress' we are exposed to pushes us to the point of feeling unable to cope with that pressure, or worse to be overwhelmed by it. Reference is made to the damaging effects (Xref. Ch 8??) which may include anxiety, lack of sleep, depression, a tendency for the immune system to be less resilient.

Let's consider that a certain amount of 'positive pressure or motivation' is what 'gets us out of bed in the morning'. Consider that driving force or 'get on with it' mode is a key to a healthier lifestyle, it 'switches you on at the start of the day' and primes you to meet the demands of the day.

Recently a study by the University of Texas discovered a link between hectic lifestyles and a superior processing speed of the brain, better reasoning and improved memory, proving that being busy keeps us 'sharp' and may even delay cognitive decline and dementia as we age.

Evolution gave us the 'fight or flight' reaction to help us survive, not to kill us. Short bursts of adrenalin help to stimulate immune activity helping the healing process and so giving us greater protection against disease. (Ref; Professor Dhabar, Researcher at Stanford University School of Medicine.) Busy people are generally less bothered by lack of sleep and enjoy as much sleep as their busy lives allow. Being active and working with horses can put us in a better mental state ready for bed and being busy can help promote sleepiness.

Boredom is rarely a word common in the vocabulary of those of us involved with horses! Think of us 'busy people with horses in our lives' as being on a moving walkway. We stay actively somewhere in the middle. Not keeping moving along that walkway, generates feelings of not achieving, boredom, maybe anxiety and becoming overwhelmed by not 'getting

anywhere'. If our environment doesn't stimulate us enough, we will become lazy and not 'get on with it'. We need stimulation to make progress, but we need to balance it against being overwhelmed.

Being 'positively busy', planning and setting realistic achievable goals, are all associated with living a longer and happier life. Balance is the key to being busy, when busy 'feels too much', then that balance of 'work/horse/life' ratio needs considering and if necessary adjusting.

Whereas in an early development sport, such as tennis or gymnastics the 'equipment' does not fundamentally change. Rings, parallel bars and a Pommel horse in gymnastics and a racquet in tennis are inanimate, therefore malfunction in equipment is manageable, usually by like for like replacement.

With horses, who are all (as we are) unique and individual, while having common characteristics. Riding therefore as a sport, requires greater adaptability and versatility, this retains our interest in the sport and constant challenge to improve.

More knowledge and experience are usually required to ride a 'hotter' horse and this often becomes easier with age and maturity. The older we get, the more we have learnt and therefore the easier we find it to learn further. (X Ref ch 11)

Dressage is not just 'riding a horse' it is knowledge and ability in training the horse, and as such is a specialism in equestrian sport. The horse now used for dressage riding is of an ever increasing quality of athleticism and expression of the basic gaits (walk, trot and canter).

Riding can be for anyone.
- One's aspiration may be to 'ride like Charlotte or Carl'. To have an iconic role model in any sport is motivating and inspirational.
- In riding horses, we must first learn to ride and then if we aspire to 'train horses', we must continue to learn to ride better and better so that we are able to understand, and correctly influence the horse, to train him with knowledge, consistency and empathy.

Variations on 'fitness'. Developing fitness through other methods.
- Fitness = the ability to be mentally and physically capable of fulfilling a task.
- To be fit enough to run a marathon is a very different level of fitness to being able to walk in a leisurely manner 200 yards to the nearest shop.
- Identifying the fitness required to ride a horse will be relevant to many factors, e.g. age, flexibility, optimum weight, past fitness history etc, etc, and then the aim with the horse, e.g. leisurely ride once a week or 50 mile Endurance ride in six months time.
- A plan is the absolute primary consideration – in this chapter we are only considering the fitness of the rider.
- Riding ensures the use of the muscles involved in balance and coordination to stay in partnership with the horse.
- We will now touch on other activities which will assist in the development of fitness and coordination that will contribute significantly to the rider's well being if they are not able to ride more than once or twice a week.

Swimming:
- Non weight baring, develops cardiovascular efficiency (breathing), suppleness, flexibility and stamina.
- An all-round muscular work out.
- Islay swims two or three times a week and believes it also gives you 'thinking time'.

Walking:
- Needing self-motivation (but so does everything!) and a dog may help!
- Can be tailored to 100 yards to infinite miles depending on time, and that self motivation again.
- It is a cost free activity that gives you 'thinking time'.
- Can develop stamina and cardiovascular expansion. (depending on the gradients you walk)
- Develops overall muscular strength and fitness.

Pilates/Equi Pilates/Yoga:

Islay has found huge benefit from Equi Pilates over the last three years. She would attribute her fitness and regular riding well being now, to the programme of Pilates training that she has followed with Veronika Mills. Here is an account from Veronika answering the questions that Islay put to her.

INTERVIEW: Veronika Mills.

Q: How did you become an Equi Pilates (Pilates) trainer?

A: When I first came to the UK I was an Au Pair-on the farm looking after children, as well as horses and other farm animals, as that's what I studied back in the Czech Republic, agriculture, horticulture and equestrian studies. I have been involved with horses since I was 11. After my Au Pair visa expired, I started to work and ride at various stables and yards. The last one before leaving the 'groom' industry was a Race yard and a Stud Farm, where I spent about 5 years. I had also been teaching at our local riding school where I had been riding since coming to the UK, as they were very close to where I lived. The reason for leaving the grooming job, was that I found it very hard on my body and I wanted to do something where I could work with people, horses and stay fit at the same time. I qualified as a Personal Trainer and Fitness Instructor and started working part time in the Gym.

I also came across an Equipilates Teacher Training Course (Equipilates TM –founded by Lindsay Wilcox-Reid) about a year into being a personal trainer, which was exactly what I had in mind in the first instance. This would enable me to work with horse riders, helping them improve their postures, riding skills, become more effective and offer them new tools on how to improve their horse related goals. As we say, 'become the rider their horse would choose'. The fitness training fits in nicely with this, as more and more people have in the last few years realized that their fitness and well being is just as important as that of their horse, in order to achieve best results.

Since then I have attended several Workshops in our Equi Pilates HQ to improve my teaching skills, use various methods and equipment to help riders improve their asymmetries, imbalances and medical issues. These often have been due to falls, other injuries or just years of focusing more on their horse than themselves.

Q: Of your regular clientele, what percentage would be under 30, how many in the 30 -50 age range, and how many over 50?

A: Around 10% are under 30, probably around 50% are in the middle age range and 40% are over 50. I have non equestrian clients as well and around half a dozen who are between 70 and 83.

Q: What changes do you see in the clients who regularly practice with you?

A: Most people notice how much their core strength has improved.

Those with mild medical conditions such as lower back pain, shoulder pain, disc pain have commented their symptoms have decreased, if not disappeared altogether, or that their condition is now manageable without pain relief.

Other changes I see is in their balance, body coordination and improving overall strength.

Many report that when their horse spooks or they go over a wrongly timed jump, before they would simply fall off but now they stay on and feel much safer.

Their confidence is improving. Sometimes a very shy and quiet client comes to my class and as the time goes by I can see how their confidence grows as they get better.

In my elderly clients, the main change I see is their confidence, in terms of strength and balance. A lot of them at the beginning of the programme will struggle or refuse to get on the floor as they worry they won't get up. After some time they are happy to sit on a Swiss ball and do exercises on the floor. They also report being steadier on their feet when walking outside or with their dogs.

Q: What are the mental and physical benefits of Pilates?

A: There are Sooooo many!

Mental:
- Improved self-awareness, self-control, motivation.
- Helps with stress, anxiety and depression management.
- Helps to focus and concentrate.
- Improving inner balance, mood - in the current world of chaos, stress and imbalance.
- Pilates will help settle a person's mind and improve well-being, this will often improve their sleep pattern.
- Pilates can also help with getting rid of bad habits, (e.g. bad posture, crossing legs when sitting, etc)

Physical:
- Improved overall muscle tone, strength, balance, coordination, make the

body more symmetrical left/right and back/front.

- Increased proprioception – person's ability to know where their body is in space, e.g. knowing if we are standing barefoot, in shoes, on grass or concrete; the ability to balance on one leg without having to look down.
- Weight loss.
- Improving medical conditions management.
- Help in recovering from an injury, surgery, pregnancy.
- Increased lung capacity and function.
- Improved central nervous system- as we learn to voluntarily engage muscles (some of which may have been 'asleep' for a while), helps to keep our nervous system healthy. This will ensure that our brain is communicating well with the rest of our body.

Q: What else can you tell me about Pilates in relevance to the older rider especially?

A: As Pilates works on posture, body awareness, breathing and core strength, this together with working on coordination and stability, can improve functional movement and prevent falls. Horse riding is going to improve all those aspects of Pilates. It's helping improve brain activity, maintain muscle tone, activity and generally keep individuals fit and healthy. It's also great for mental health, getting out in fresh air and socializing with other like-minded people – who love horses.

I would say 90% of my clients are still actively riding, either for pleasure or competitively and I love seeing them do it. It's great to see their determination and passion for it, and the attitude that they won't give up.

Q: My final question to Veronika was to ask her if there were any other comments or information she wanted to share:

A: "I think participating in Equi Pilates gives people more to think about and to focus on themselves as well as their horse. The great thing about it is that we can take all the movements the human body goes through whilst on the horse, off the horse, take them apart and work on each aspect of that movement separately. We can then find out where the body might have some asymmetries, imbalances or restrictions and with a carefully planned programme (with the help of some other health professionals such as physios, sport massage people and others), we can help 're-programme' some unwanted postural patterns so that the body can function correctly again. I have clients from all walks of life and usually with multiple injuries from past riding accidents and it's very rewarding to see their progress and especially when they say they thought they would never get better again or that they would have to live with that chronic pain forever.

Sometimes it's the simplest of things that will achieve the biggest results."

Reflections:
- 'Horses for life' resonates throughout this chapter.
- No one could fail to be moved by the two interviews from riders who were severely injured (while riding their beloved horses), but whose drive to return to the saddle overwhelmed everything. The horse became the focus of their recovery and continues to sustain their 'raison d'etre'.

- Ownership of horses conveys a fundamental commitment to activity (care, management, training and riding) on a daily basis.
- That involvement with the horse may slip in and out of our life's progression. It may be absent for months or in some cases years, but it usually infiltrates back in, at some period of our lives. It may never have been part of your life, but it is never too late to start and to realise a long-held dream or passion to have 'horses in your life'.

Summary:
Link some of the contents of this chapter to 'Where is the beginning' and 'Maintaining rider well being' and we are continuing to build a picture of 'horses for life'. Still to come will be chapters that highlight the horse's role in today's society and into the future. Please keep reading.

Islay Auty on 'Lowry'

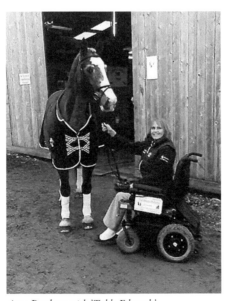

Anne Dunham with 'Teddy Edwards'

Jonty Evans on 'Cooley Rorkes Drift' (aka 'Art')

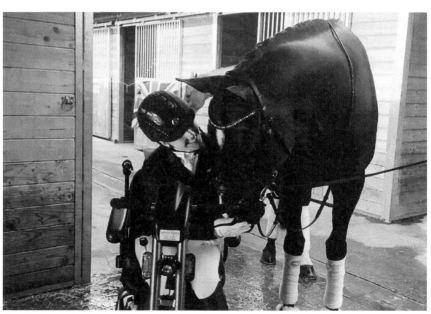

Suzi Hext with 'Abira'

Pammy Hutton on 'Amanti'

Suzi Hext with 'Abira' ('Empathy!')

Pammy Hutton on 'Avalon' ('Balance or not')

Emile Faurie Foundation 'EFF'

Emile Faurie Foundation 'EFF'

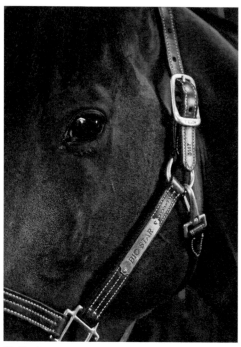

Big Star!

CHAPTER EIGHT

THE HORSE'S ROLE IN LIFE TODAY:

KEY POINTS:
- Therapeutic value of horses
- Emile Faurie Foundation. (E.F.F.)
- British Horse Society Changing Lives Through Horses
- Unique Interviews/Case studies
- Riding for the Disabled (RDA)
- Bringing horses into the lives of people to help them with self awareness, self discovery and renewal

- Anxiety; Stress; PTSD (Post Traumatic Stress Disorder); Depression; Feeling Fear;
- Managing pain; Addiction; Anorexia Nervosa/Bulimia Nervosa; OCD (Obsessive Compulsive Disorder)
- Autism
- Bereavement
- Rehabilitation of offenders or those alienated from society
- Eva Hamilton Key 4 Life programme.

- 'Being' with horses, allows us to learn from them. Horses 'live completely in the moment'. They have no ability to think forward 'what will tomorrow bring?' They have minimal ability to think about 'yesterday' or 'last week' in the way that we do. Their 'memory' may relate to a past experience, but they do not 'remember and reflect' about life as we do. Their memory comes into play when that past experience is revisited, then they remember and react in the way that they did on the first occasion of that experience.

- No horse will return to his stable thinking to himself 'I must work on my suppleness in the lateral work'!!

- Reflection is predominantly a human thought process.

- Horses are non-judgemental, they are 'followers not leaders' they 'put up with many injustices from us' – some not intended and some sadly intentional.

- Horses are a mirror of us. If we are nervous the horse will be nervous, cheerful and the horse will be cheerful, depressed and the horse will reflect that, angry and the horse will be angry. React quickly with lack of 'feel' and the horse will too. Frustration, irritation and anger are human emotions that all too frequently we transfer to the unsuspecting horse.

- To enhance our relationship with the horse, we must learn to 'think like a horse' and control our human emotions and reactions when with him. The horse does not choose to work with us, although in most situations he is a willing and enthusiastic partner. He must be trained with an understanding of how he learns, which is by repetition and memory. It is our responsibility to ensure that the information we convey to him is clear, consistent and well timed.

This Chapter will highlight some of the phenomenal roles that the horse is now capable of fulfilling in the lives of children and adults, for whom life has dealt a variety of disadvantages.

Emile Faurie Foundation (EFF): Reaching children through horses
Emile is a leading International Dressage rider and Trainer who successfully runs a training competition yard in the Cotswolds, and has represented GB at World, European and Olympic Championships, winning 4 European medals including Team Gold in 2011 and World Silver in 2018.

He is passionate about all children being able to experience the joy of horses and his vision was to start his own foundation, providing funds to make this possible. **The Emile Faurie Foundation was created in 2006.** It aims to transform the lives of hundreds of disadvantaged children and young people, who live in Inner cities and poor areas of the UK, by giving them the opportunity to experience the joy of caring for and riding horses.

Since its inception the EFF has funded projects helping over 12,000 children and young people. Money raised goes directly to help these youngsters to ride and be involved with horse care. It improves their confidence, self-esteem and life skills. This in turn helps them to achieve more at school, improve their health and wellbeing, avoid slipping into gang culture or crime and, in some cases, gives them a focus for a career in due course in the horse industry. Contact with the horse also has therapeutic benefits to those with behavioural problems and special needs due to their personal circumstances.

Some quotes from those children involved:
- "Horses bring peace in my life"

- "I forget my problems at home, and I know I would like to work with horses in the future."
- "The Foundation is like my island, it keeps me afloat, without it I would sink."
- "I was heading for trouble – gangs, drugs, truancy, when through the EFF I found horses. My life has changed dramatically, and I cannot thank you enough for this amazing opportunity."

EFF states: "Learning to ride is a life changing experience for so many people, and even more so for those children and young people who are disadvantaged through poverty, neglect or harm."

Using the following acronym clearly identifies the extensive role of this worthwhile and far reaching foundation:

R: Realises these childrens' dreams giving them the opportunity to experience being with horses.

I: Improves their self-esteem and confidence enabling them to improve their work at school and helps them achieve.

D: Develops their social skills helping them with relationships with their teachers and other children, preventing some getting into trouble through gangs, truancy and drugs.

E: Encourages good behaviour and helps to deal with anxiety and stress related problems, giving them a healthy, safe environment outside school and home to ENJOY themselves.

(www.emilefauriefoundation.org.uk)

THE BRITISH HORSE SOCIETY - Changing Lives Through Horses.
This programme was set up to address the needs of the 10% or more young people between the ages of 16 - 24 who are no longer in any form of education, training or employment. Often these young people have given up and lost any focus they may have had to strive to achieve into the future. It is known that one in ten children in society now have a recognised mental health issue, and that increases to one in five young adults.

The aim of Changing Lives Through Horses is to help give those young people disengaged from Society the opportunity to develop skills to facilitate their return to education or employment.

This book has already highlighted the powerful impact that horses can have on those disadvantaged by the trials and knocks of life. Horses are non-judgemental, they have no awareness of the background of any of the people they meet young or old. The contact with horses then becomes the inspiration to these youngsters for change.

This programme shows young people how to develop key skills that will sustain them in the future. They are taught life skills that will provide a lifelong provision for a viable future. The key skills of Communication, Confidence, Teamwork, Relationships, Responsibility and Personal Achievement transform the lives of those participating to give them aspiration, and a genuine sense of respect, for the horse and themselves. They can 'dare to dream' and many then go on and choose to work with horses as a career option. One young person who benefited from the programme, which is run in British Horse Society Approved Riding Establishments, said: "It hasn't made my life, it has changed my life".

- In the 21st Century and in our technological world we are bombarded with information which has in many situations overwhelmed our fundamental 'fight or flight response'. It often puts us into a permanent state of heightened awareness or 'flight'. Adrenalin is running and this raises heart rate and respiration which puts the body in a state of high alert unnecessarily. This exerts stress on our normal body functioning and can in the longer term create a semi chronic (or uncontrollable) sense of anxiety, stress, fear and depression.
- We would re-emphasise here, as in other chapters that our experience, guidance and any suggestions made, are delivered from two highly experienced professionals in the horse industry. We do not intend to give any medical advice for individuals who may be suffering from clinical conditions that require professional advice or help from trained medics.

The brevity of the information we share with you here, is in no way an indication of a lack of huge importance that needs to be the consideration of the conditions to which we refer. We mention these conditions in relation to the relevance that they may have, in touching the lives of anyone working in the demanding environment of the horse industry in the 21st Century. The horse industry can and should provide an uplifting, challenging, exciting and fulfilling occupation for anyone who loves horses. We recognise however that this may not always be the case. We hope that this chapter may help develop awareness within employers and employees, to help both, in overcoming the potential for a break down in wellbeing of either. Thus providing a source of awareness, resulting in a cohesive pathway of understanding for all.

Riding for the Disabled (Association) RDA:

This amazing organisation was founded in 1965 with nine member groups initially called the 'Advisory Council on Riding for the Disabled'. By 1969 it had grown to 80 member groups and became the 'Riding for the Disabled Association'. The Association has for over fifty years recognised the therapeutic value of riding. It had as its first President, Lavinia Duchess of Norfolk and HRH Princess Anne as its Patron. HRH the Princess Royal is a past European Eventing Individual Gold medalist (1971) and Mother of Zara Tindall (European Eventing Champion 2005 and World Eventing Champion 2005 & 2006, among a plethora of Team medals at European, World and Olympic level.)

In 1976 HRH Princess Anne, the Princess Royal, became the President of RDA, a position she still holds today. HRH herself has a lifelong involvement with horses. This organisation is run almost entirely by volunteers. From small beginnings, the philosophy of recognising the therapeutic benefits of riding horses for people with disabilities, has developed into a nationwide organisation that delivers fun, activities, learning and therapeutic development to children and adults, with a huge range of mental and physical disabilities. Riding for the Disabled has provided countless people with disability a mobility and freedom through riding, that would otherwise have confined them to a wheelchair or limited mobility. (X.Ref: Ch 3. Ch 7)

The organisation which thrives throughout the UK, is a triumph of riding schools offering facilities and safe horses, for children and adults, to benefit from the relationship with the horse. Pammy is proud to know that her family establishment, Talland School of Equitation, is one of the oldest school's providing Riding for the Disabled. Riding for the Disabled also has a huge family of volunteers who willingly give up time on a regular basis to lead horses, offering support to severely disabled riders. They gain camaraderie and huge satisfaction from their involvement in an organisation that provides such amazing opportunities to a wide range of people with disability. It is widely considered that volunteering is a hugely beneficial way of improving loneliness, mental wellbeing and physical health, especially if the physical commitment is in leading horses for riders with disability and generally being active in the management and caring for such riders and the horses they ride. In a survey done by the RDA for its 50th anniversary last year, more than 1600 of its 18,000 volunteers were questioned and 81% said volunteering made them feel better about themselves, 84% felt more cheerful and 92% felt more useful, (Horse and Hound Feb 7th 2020). The

RDA is pushing for more recognition of the 'dual benefit' to the volunteers and to the community they support.

Ed Bracher: CEO of the Riding for the Disabled Association
Islay was privileged to have a fascinating conversation with Ed Bracher, which revealed the following facts:
Q. What is the ongoing aim for RDA?
A. Always to help facilitate a disabled person linking with the benefits of contact with a horse. This initial link could lead to a future Paralympian rider but just as important is recognising the value of the horse and enabling a person (often a child or young person) to experience a 'horse fix' for someone who 'just wants to be with a horse'.
Q. Why and how is the role of the volunteer so important?
A. There is a dual role of sense of personal 'feeling good about themselves' for the volunteer but also the fact that they are fulfilling a valuable role in helping the rider. It's the ability to link up with disabled riders in a meaningful way.
Q. Are there still plenty of volunteers available?
A. There is a concern that there are fewer volunteers or that the average age of the volunteer is increasing but that is not borne out by statistics. Volunteers are enthusiastic and involved, but sometimes reluctant to take on roles of responsibility (e.g. chairman or secretary of a local group)
Q. What is the link between RDA and Paralympic Dressage?
A. In London 2012 (Olympics) all the Para team had started their riding lives in RDA. After London there was a definite rise in RDA riders wanting to compete. One of the things that makes GB so successful in Paralympic Dressage is the strength of the origins of riders through the RDA. So often a rider will say 'when I'm on a horse I don't feel disabled', or 'when I'm on a horse I can look down on other people, usually I have to look up as they are looking down on me.' These are powerful statements reflecting the inclusivity that 'the horse' can provide to the disabled person.
Q. Are there any threats to the ongoing success of RDA and how can these be alleviated?
A. Understanding the horse's role in therapy was recognised in the early 1960s. Pioneers of the benefits were emphasised by Stella Saywell, a Physiotherapist from Bristol and equestrians like Sheila Shore, Jane Wykeham-Musgrave and Sister Chiara (formerly Cherry Hatton Hall FBHS). A Danish rider Lis Hartell competed at the Helsinki Olympics

1952 where, as a polio sufferer which had caused her to be severely disabled, she competed against able bodied riders and men for the first time to win an Individual Silver medal. This was repeated at the Melbourne games of 1956 (equestrian events were held in Stockholm due to Australia's strict quarantine rules). The RDA was initially driven by the massive impact and determination of people like these.

Today disability is much more recognised, especially in sport overall and on the whole, there are far more opportunities for disabled riders, including competition. Often disabled people get involved with horses in other ways rather than through RDA centres. but the majority of people who come to RDA have had no previous background with horses. Physical disability is well accepted these days but now there is an increase in those coming to RDA with mental disabilities or learning difficulties, these are sometimes not so well accepted if not clearly understood.

We have recently developed a scheme for older people with dementia – 'Tea with a pony' is obviously not about riding but it is impactful in the ability of people having a good experience with a horse or pony. Our role is linking up skilled people and horses with the ability to give disadvantaged people a meaningful empathy with 'the horse'.

§

- Many of our Paralympic riders who started their riding experience in their local RDA Group, gained their feeling of independence and ability to move into competitive riding and have gone on to national and international achievements.
- Anne Dunham (featured In ch. 3) achieved multiple Paralympic, World and European medals from 1996 (when Paralympic Dressage first featured at The Atlanta USA games) until 2016. In 2012 at the London Olympics, all five members of Team GB who won Team Gold, started their riding careers with RDA (Sophie Christianson CBE, Sir Lee Pearson, Sophie Wells MBE, Debbie Criddle MBE, Natasha Baker MBE).

§

Pammy teaches a young man who's existence has been an ongoing permanent struggle with the life threatening condition Cystic Fibrosis. His account is one of unbelievable courage and is moving beyond words.

CASE STUDY:

Patrick suffers from Cystic Fibrosis – a progressive genetic disease that causes persistent lung infections and is debilitating over time limiting the person's ability to breathe. This is his personal account:

"The one thing to be said about insomnia is that it creates more hours to get things done!

I am 38 this summer. My Mother was told not to expect me to live beyond the age of seven, then it was eleven, then eighteen. Current expectations from 'my team' was that in 2018 I had a less than 50% chance of making it to 2020. The short answer now is no-one has a clue on life expectancy as a result of the surprising effectiveness of new drugs. We didn't think they would work on my problems at all but I'm still here! No-one knows with my complications but possibly a few years? One bad infection will kill me.

I had ridden since my teens but as both I and my horses got older, I was able to do less and less as my lung function got poorer and poorer. In addition, since my early 20's we had known that I had brittle bones due to osteoporosis and that one bad fall would shatter me like a china doll. Things deteriorated to the point where one day I had to admit defeat. My old event horse had always been 'enthusiastic' to hack and there was the day when I had to get off and ring the yard to come and pick us up from a field as I had nearly collapsed off the horse as I couldn't breathe. It was a low point. Shortly after that day I had a severe chest infection that turned very quickly into pneumonia and respiratory failure. After 7 weeks in hospital I was discharged. I stayed out of hospital for 4 days before a major artery in my lungs exploded and I was fortunate to be near the hospital or it is doubtful I would have survived. Over the next few months, this repeated, to a greater or lesser extent, every few days. As a result I was sent for transplant assessment, but unfortunately because of an old riding injury and my low bone density, I wasn't eligible for listing.

At this point it became obvious that I didn't need to 'preserve myself' in anticipation of a call for transplantation and so once the bleeding had finally started to settle SLIGHTLY, I gave in and went to Talland. We had no idea what getting on a horse would do to my lungs, even just in walk, we also had no idea how they would respond. I made this explicitly clear to Pammy, but the urge to ride was sufficient to overcome a large amount of fear, because life isn't worth it if your are only existing, you need to be living! - Nothing happened! Before 'getting on' I told my doctors about the possibility of riding again. While at no point could they recommend it, they didn't tell me explicitly no. I think because they knew I was very likely to ignore them anyway. The stubborn streak that had kept me going through the difficult times could also cause the Doctors and I to butt heads.

Over the coming months we gradually increased the amount that I did on Pammy's horses. As we did, the urge to try getting back on board my own old boy grew. We had no idea what would happen if I tried to get back on after two years. As I say, he had always been very sharp to ride and we just didn't know how he would respond. Pammy and I discussed how we could do it as safely as possible and eventually the urge became too great to ignore. While the doctors recognised the potential benefit to my mental health of riding him again, they were extremely concerned about something negative happening, they knew the horse had a reputation. . As soon as I sat on him however, I knew it was worth the risk. . It was like putting on old comfortable slippers. It just felt right. The horse didn't put a single foot wrong. We were only supposed to have a small walk, but we were frankly never going to obey that! We had a little trot and I felt the stress and tensions draining away. I described it to people just as two best mates going to the pub for a beer and reliving past glories. Everyone who knew me could see the change in me.

*The risk from me riding was very real, frankly we were all geared up for it to go wrong. The doctors were very supportive of me trying, but it was obvious that they felt it was very risky. From a purely medical and physical point of view they would have preferred it didn't happen. I was lucky they understood that, especially for someone who has many more years behind them than in front of them, being in a position of being able to do the one thing that brought me calm, peace and a huge sense of enjoyment was important. I live with chronic pain issues all day every day, from chest pain and whole body pain from the C.F. to nerve damage in my spine from a climbing accident, through to sciatica caused by low body weight causing nerve pinching. I have lived with chronic pain for years, going back to when I was eventing. I later discovered that I had spent the latter half of a season eventing with a fractured sternum that never healed. Pain is something you like to imagine that you will always beat when it isn't too bad. If pain builds, it will try and stop you doing everything you love. **The fear of that pain is as destructive as pain itself. So as well as trying to overcome the pain, sufferers must try to overcome the fear.** I don't manage this every day, I applaud people who do. I used to pride myself on being mentally strong but alas sometimes we discover we aren't as strong as we wish to be.*

§

Anxiety:

Anxiety can be defined as a feeling of worry or unease in one's circumstances or current situation. It creates a state of inner turmoil within the sufferer. The sufferer may worry or even dread impending events.

Anxiety is a natural response of the brain to a stimulus of something that could damage the individual – it is a response to 'fear'. Fear exists, either as a past experience and is due to the threat of danger, pain or harm, or a new experience, to which there is an instinctive response. Once the brain has identified this stimulus as a past experience, the 'thinking brain' can then re- focus on these thoughts and magnify them.

Allowed to develop, these feelings can become prevailing on a daily basis or whenever the individual is in a situation that highlights or focuses on the cause of the anxiety, e.g. with a student rider anxiety about riding a particular horse (on which they may have already had a bad experience), taking a practical exam for which they feel apprehensive, ill prepared or nervous. Unfortunately, because the horse will have no similar awareness of the exam day or the apprehension of the candidate, the situation may become a 'self-fulfilling prophecy'! Consider this situation:

- Rider anxious and nervous about their capability for the impending situation where their riding will be under scrutiny.
- For the horse – another day of going into the arena to be ridden.
- Tense rider worrying rather than concentrating positively on the systematic calm riding of the horse.
- Horse feels the rider's anxiety and lack of leadership, so the horse reacts by spooking or becoming tense, which exacerbates an already anxious situation, potentially causing a deteriorating situation. Horses spook when they are not 'on the aids', they are not following

primarily the leadership of the rider. If the rider is anxious then the horse will register the lack of leadership of the rider and 'choose his own agenda' – usually a spook or adverse reaction. This confirms the rider's anxiety which becomes worse – a 'vicious circle of expectation and self-fulfilling prophecy' for the rider.

Q: Are these feelings normal?
A: Yes, quite normal for most people, at any stage of their lives.
Q: Are these feelings manageable?
A: Yes, in the first instance.
Q: How?
A: Good training of horse and rider, understanding of the perspective of the 'anxiety' from both rider and coach.

Simple exercises can help the person to manage anxiety in the first instance, but as with any new skill these exercises need to be practised so that they serve as the defence mechanism.

- Commit your anxieties to paper – write them down and read them – then identify 'why' they worry you and talk through the management of that worry with a trusted friend, mentor, or your instructor, if it is horse related.
- Breathing exercises can help. Start at the base of your little finger with the other index finger, breathe in and trace your finger up the little finger, breathe out and trace down the little finger, breathe in and trace up your fourth finger, breathe out and down the fourth finger, continue until you have completed all your fingers and thumb. You should find that your brain has adapted to the breathing and feeling (not the focus of your anxiety) so your anxiety is reduced. Consider the feeling of that reduction and **take ownership of it - you have produced it -** your brain, complex though it is, actually thrives on concentrating on **one or two key things at a time.** Use this breathing exercise (or something similar) before you go to **'face your fear'**.
- Wherever you are, when the anxiety begins to grip you, go and find a horse, groom him, just be with him and enjoy the horse and use breathing to regulate your anxiety, concentrate on the ability to draw life giving breath into your body and control the exhalation. **Feel** (X.ref ch 2) the strength of being in control of every breath and gradually build that into the situation that promotes your anxiety. You are in control and through focus and good practise of breathing, you can increasingly banish the 'fear response' in your thinking brain and replace it with your 'strength response'.

Stress:
Defined as: A state of mental or emotional strain or tension resulting from adverse or demanding circumstances. Something that causes strain or tension. Become tense or anxious.

Stress is a word that is much more current in our day to day vocabulary now than five decades ago. It is used in equestrian terms also to describe putting the horse under unnecessary or inappropriate pressure. In this context therefore, we can relate back to that essential empathy or feeling that should exist between the horse and rider in that two-way relationship.

Stress is defined as a build-up of strain and pressure, and in many sporting situations it is seen as a 'positive'. It can heighten motivation and develop or raise sporting performance. Too much of anything however can have negative effects. A build-up of the pressures and strains of life in general can therefore create a destructive environment, where an individual ceases to cope with the pressure, which is then generalised and attributed to 'stress'.

In today's world, young people often refer to being 'stressed' in situations that bear no relation to the circumstances that a young fighter pilot during

the second world war would find himself in. Barely out of his teenage years, he may have been fighting for his life for King and Country in a tiny aircraft above the English Channel.

Relatively for both individuals the intensity of their 'stress' is very real. In the first instance something as minor as being unable to complete a required task in training or at work (handing in an assignment on time, preparing a horse to travel and leaving on time) can generate emotions of panic, insecurity and failure. In the second situation, the young pilot would be acting and reacting instantaneously to survive, with no time to 'dwell' on feelings at the time, but after may reflect intensely on the circumstances endured. In hindsight the young man's stress may become extremely tangible and invasive. With repeated exposure to the intensity of stress that this scenario highlights, linked with the likelihood that the pilot may survive while experiencing the loss of colleagues and friends, **PTSD (Post Traumatic Stress Disorder)** may become a resulting condition.

Post-Traumatic Stress Disorder:
PTSD is described as a disorder brought about by an individual's exposure to injury or severe psychological shock.

The individual is likely to become withdrawn from others, suffer sleep disturbance and a tendency to suffer vivid recall of the experience. Often associated with ex-service personnel, nevertheless PTSD can manifest symptoms in civilians who have experienced a traumatic event, e.g. a severe car crash or riding accident. PTSD would not frequently be associated with equestrian sport. It is an isolating and intensely personal condition affecting every individual differently. It is terrifying in its ability to overwhelm the sufferer during the night through nightmares and irrational feelings of being under threat. It is vital for anyone who may be suffering in silence, trying to overcome the 'demons', or attempting to shield their family or nearest and dearest from what they consider to be a personal problem, that they seek support from health professionals and preferably, if necessary, approach an organisation that specialises in the help and management required to overcome this limiting state of mind. (e.g. 'Combat Stress')

Fear:

Fear is defined as a feeling of anxiety concerning the outcome of something or someone's safety. The likelihood of something unwelcome happening. An unpleasant emotion caused by the threat of danger, pain or harm.

There is probably not a person involved with horses who at some time in their life has not experienced 'fear'.

That adrenalin rush that immerses your body and senses in an instant, causes your heart to race and your hands to go clammy. Then, depending on the time span and resulting ability to identify the cause of the fear, it is usually possible to manage the fear and turn the body's natural automatic response into semi-controlled or controlled decision making to deal with the cause.

Fear as a rider, can be an inhibitor to progress. As already mentioned, the horse is a mirror of our mental state, so if we are fearful that is easily conveyed to the horse. The horse needs leadership, fear will limit decision making and leadership, and the resulting indecision of the partnership becomes a miss match of tension and loss of harmony between horse and rider.

- As a rider be courageous enough to identify your lack of confidence, share that anxiety with a friend or even better with your instructor/coach.
- Recognising and taking ownership of your own fear is a big step towards managing it.
- An understanding and experienced instructor will support your courage in admitting a fear and help to rationalise it, make a plan for managing it and putting in place steps to overcome it.

FEELING FEAR

Pammy's account:

At this time in my life, I have a mare who is 8 years old and I had put off riding and schooling her, let alone all the training she needs. She is 17 hh and can buck, and it was that buck that made me nervous as I so nearly fell off her as a five year old. The reminder will still be there in years to come as she hit and scratched the mirror in the indoor school.

How hard it is to admit how absolutely terrified I am of falling off. Being a rider now that is riding against doctor's orders, if I had another fall, what is left of my back would pack up. I ride her frightened and almost suffering from vertigo – certainly due to high blood pressure I get dizzy.

The cure was in perseverance. I ride her every day now, and every day I tell myself to 'shut up', and every day we improve a bit together. Only the new things make me frightened. The new piaffe, the new one-time changes. The best news of all is that I am fitter than I have been for years, to ride my older Grand Prix horses. Actually, the better news is that she might make grand prix. So, I have just bought a six year old and now for the next one I am 'off the walls frightened'!

The life lesson has only been the understanding of how to get over fear and how much the mind set can hold you back. The sense of achievement is second to none, as my young horses improve. Wow, still to be able to feel at one with a horse, that is worth all the work and effort. The extraordinary thing is that before I decided to re-start with the mare, Islay had fallen in love with her and always rides her on visits to me, and out on courses with top trainers. To be sharing a horse is amazing. To be feeling the same emotions through a horse is staggering.

Islay's account:

I spent nearly four years not riding (X Ref Author's profiles) because my back surgery had left me with minimal feeling and effect down my left leg, due to severe damage to the sciatic nerve. I sold my last horse, who I had taken from novice to Prix St. George level, as I was convinced that I couldn't ride him to do him justice any more. My surgeon had said "don't ride for four months, and then you can ride again". So that's what I did. What I did not build into that statement, of course, was "you will have to learn to ride again and retrain your horse to understand your left leg no longer functions the way it did!" I rode less and less and missed riding more and more. One day I remember having a 'light bulb moment' where my brain told me that I had gone into horses as a career all those years ago because of my love of riding. I was now a competent coach with increased skill because I no longer 'could just have a sit on to show my pupils', so why on earth had I given up the greatest fun and joy of all – the riding! I rang Pammy and said "I'm thinking of starting to ride again!" In typical Pammy manner "She said come over tomorrow!" I went, and with her typical generosity she put me on one of her lovely trained horses. I was weak, uncoordinated, insecure and the poor horse 'put up with me'. Eventually I made some semblance of riding him in a balanced and connected fashion and my day was completely made. Since that day, some years ago, I go regularly to Talland and have gradually and systematically rebuilt my riding fitness and ability. In conjunction with Pilates, (X Ref. Ch 6) swimming two or three times a week and riding a client's event horses twice a week, I now ride probably better (mentally) than I ever have. Feeling fear – yes I too was horribly aware that I had not fallen off since having my back fixed and that a fall would not be in my best interests. One winter's day when riding on my own outdoors in a sand school, the horse and I had a difference in opinion of where we were going, and I ended up on the floor with the horse looking startled and apologetic that we had parted company. To my delight I was unhurt, remounted and suffered no after-effects at all. That too for me was a barrier that needed to be crossed. It is to be avoided, and can be minimised by relevant management, but it is not completely unavoidable, just as climbing up a ladder, running downstairs and driving one's car carries inherent risk of mishap.

I have been so fortunate to develop a super rapport with Pammy's mare. It is quite thrilling to ride such a lovely, sensitive, horse and find that unique harmony and feel with her. Pammy has been so generous in allowing me to 'share' the horse on the occasions that I go down to Talland. My highlights have been attending the annual two-day course of the Fellows and Instructor's of the BHS (F and I Association) with Adam Kemp FBHS, and a training session with Emile Faurie.

LIVING WITH PAIN.
Pammy's account:

Living with pain is for me an 'always'. It is just a question of how much pain each and every day? At the last visit to my Doctor, he asked if I wanted a disabled badge for my car yet. He wants me to stop riding and walking as soon as possible. How can a person who loves horses and lives for horses do that? (X.Ref. Suzi Hext Ch 6) I wake up and almost can't walk to the kettle and wait an hour for the pain killers to kick in. Every day by about 10am the pain recedes, and I feel two decades younger. That's it, all systems go! Just some days I have to bite the bullet and ride until I get through the pain. I have a pain barrier, my eyes water and the sweat starts. I can shake – and not from pop music – just sometimes it reduces me to a few tears, (I always pray no one talks to me then!) but if I can keep going somehow there is the other side, the sun comes out and I feel three decades younger. I don't look it, but I feel it! There is absolutely nothing like the feeling of being one with a horse. This does not always happen, and I feel lucky in my later life to have found another horse to bond with.

Islay's account:

Living with pain is probably an occupational hazard for most riders. My Father (Dr. X.Ref author's profile) used to say to me "you will pay for this with your back in your forties" and he was right of course! Countless falls off young and badly behaved horses, years of physical work, e.g. carrying hay on my back to ponies in a field, took its toll on my back eventually. My Father was right (as they usually are!) Often I would 'pay lip service' to good management of my own physical state, while ensuring any horses in my care were managed with the utmost regard and efficiency for their health and fitness. As the condition of my back gradually deteriorated and I increasingly suffered pain in my lower back eventually I took medical advice. I was advised that I had the worst prolapsed disc my Consultant had seen in recent times. "Surgery is your only option Mrs Auty." I said, "no chance" and staggered out of the consultation. Stubborn as a mule, I flew to Hong Kong to teach for two weeks. During that time, I could barely sit down, certainly couldn't lie down and the only position where my pain was slightly reduced was kneeling in a crawling position on all fours. I lived on strong pain killers, with intermittent sleep, in my kneeling position propped up on pillows. An eleven hour flight home had me in tears at the back of the plane after less than an hour, wondering how I would endure another 10 hours to get back to the UK. Within a week of returning home I had surgery on my prolapsed disc, and have been fortunate to be pain free since.

Countless riders in all areas of our industry suffer repeated falls and injuries (consider National Hunt jockeys). We are a stoic, stubborn lot innately and develop a resilience that sustains us through the physical and mental demands of our way of life.

Throughout this book in the personal accounts you will read of stubbornness, resilience, inner strength and a remarkable work ethic, all for the 'love of the horse'.

ADDICTION:

The definition of addiction is: To be inclined towards a particular substance (drugs, alcohol, cigarettes, chocolate) to the point that the addict is powerless to live without their addiction.

The substance becomes an invasive and often destructive part of their life, as they are unable to contemplate managing without it. Sufferers of addiction may try to hide their 'habit' from their nearest and dearest, in fear of their judgement. This can plunge them into an isolation that confirms their addiction, rather than share it, which may assist in dealing with it.

Without belittling the destructive, dire and often crippling effects of a confirmed addiction, all of us that have horses in our lives (here we mean full time) are 'addicted' to horses. We would find it difficult to live without them. This means that we have 'addictive' tendencies. It is possible for a person to be drawn into a position where the compulsion to use the source of addiction (alcohol, chocolate, cigarettes) overcomes the rational thinking or management of the mind. Maintaining the equilibrium to be able to balance the intake of the substance, in the knowledge that in excess it could do more harm than good. A tendency towards an addictive substance is more intense when the person is tired, depressed or anxious. (XRef: Ch 6 Maintaining wellbeing)

- An addiction can be an inhibitor to your personal career goals. Excess of anything –especially drugs and alcohol – will inevitably limit a clear and balanced progression in your career in the horse industry.
- An addiction can become a drain, not only on mental coping but on your financial status, which in turn can lead to greater worries, a sense of withdrawal from friends and further isolation.
- Addictions inevitably render the victim to be unreliable at times and this is a serious barrier to good training, employment or competitive aspirations.
- Take ownership at the earliest opportunity and seek support from a trusted friend or mentor, if necessary be supported to accept professional help.
- Sharing 'the problem' can involve a balanced input 'from someone who

has your best interests at heart' and will look objectively at a plan to move you gradually towards managing your craving, whatever that might be.

Anorexia Nervosa and Bulimia Nervosa:
These two psychological conditions are more often associated with young women. Described as 'eating disorders', opinions vary about whether there is a genetic predisposition towards these conditions, or whether they are triggered by environmental or cultural circumstances (occupations such as modelling, dancing or athletics often expect svelte like participants). An obsession to maintain a body image in keeping with the individual's comparison to their peer group or role model, may tip them over the edge of eating rationally, into an increased sensitivity to their weight and over-regulating a balanced food approach.

Anorexia: is symptomised by the individual considering they are overweight and becoming obsessive about losing weight. They carry out extensive food restriction, often hiding the extent to which they are starving themselves. They highly value 'being thin' often denying the fact that they are normal or underweight already.

Bulimia: is characterised by 'binge' eating to excess and usually, quickly followed by enforced vomiting or the taking of laxatives to void the body of the input. It can also be brought about by cultural pressures to conform to a 'body type' or 'image'.

Fatigue, depression and/or isolation from family or friends may cause the individual to seek food as a comfort or support but then quickly punish themselves for their self perceived weakness or dislike of 'how fat they are'.

Sharing one's feelings is fundamental to support and self-help. As an owner/manager/senior in charge of junior staff or students, it is wise to stay aware of the potential vulnerability of younger members of the team and attentive to their personal sense of self-esteem and wellbeing. A friend of Islay's who suffered both conditions in her youth said that while counselling facilitated some rehabilitation, it was the sharing experiences with others suffering the same problems, that was the turning point in support to overcome the conditions which are often closely related.

Early signs of a predisposition towards some of the issues described in this book can ensure the mental wellbeing of all individuals involved in a 'life with horses'. We can have a **shared** responsibility for ourselves and those around us, to greatly enhance the benefits of 'horses for life'.

Obsessive Compulsive Disorder:
A mental disorder, symptomised by uncontrollable, repetitive, thoughts and compulsive routines. In its worst form it can be an overwhelming condition which exhausts the sufferer, as they try to carry on with a life of normality.

Islay has a young relative who was diagnosed in early childhood and it has 'controlled' her throughout her school years, to a point where she felt she was consumed by the condition. Bravely she fund-raised, and spoke in her school assembly, to highlight the uncontrollable feelings that invade her mind while she is working hard at her normal school commitments. Cognitive Behaviour Therapy is used to some effect and there is increasing sympathy and support available to sufferers. It is seen as a lifelong condition although the sufferer learns to manage or mask the inconveniences of the effects.

As riders we may say we are a 'bit OCD' about certain routines and rituals that we adopt prior to competing. Take great care with this random use of the term 'OCD', as the mental disorder that is truly a 'different wiring of the brain' for some individuals, is an exhausting, punishing and potentially overwhelming condition, over which the individual sufferer has little control.

Riders can have a tendency towards addiction in many of the 'rituals' that they may adopt before a competition. Not only riders but many athletes in all sports will have a 'repetitive system' that they follow before any competition. This may include specific clothes, put on in a pre-determined order. 'Lucky' socks or a certain pair of breeches which must be worn, may be part of the rider's preparation. Sometimes a specific piece of music must be used to 'get the competitor in the right zone'. All these habits are acceptable, as long as failure to fulfil any of them is then not attributed to the lack of success of the competitor on the day. In that case the 'ritual' then is **destructive** rather than **constructive.** In deference to the souls that actually are afflicted by the mental disorder that is OCD, perhaps state that you are a bit 'obsessive' about something instead.

Autism:
Autism is a lifelong developmental disability that affects people in the way they perceive the world and react within it and can include problems with communication and behaviour.

It can manifest itself in a range of different ways and therefore a spectrum of symptoms can be observed which may differ greatly between two individuals diagnosed as 'autistic'. Focusing on finding a way to best meet the needs of the individual is more important than giving the symptoms a 'name'. Diagnosis from a health professional is a fundamental priority. Individuals can feel ill at ease in a variety of situations, especially those that are unfamiliar to them. This can provoke unexpected or irrational behaviour which may cause concern to those around, who are unaware of the sufferer's autism. Working with horses, or being in an environment with horses, can promote a relaxation and calming effect on the autistic individual. Interaction with horses as therapy has proved highly successful in treating those with a range of autistic symptoms.

Bereavement:
One definite fact in this life, is that at some time in our lives we will all suffer bereavement.

The death of a close member of the family or a friend, can precipitate the devastation that loss promotes. The subsequent grief (intense sorrow) that this causes can have a short, or long-term, effect on those left behind. It is still a subject that, in spite of us all knowing we will have to go through it, and will most probably have experienced in some way or other already, we can be incredibly unprepared for it, especially sudden and unexpected.

We tend to ignore it or avoid it (until it happens) and then may be woefully unable to cope with its drastic implications. Even the death of a much-loved animal or horse with whom we have had an enduring partnership, can catapult us into a black hole of misery and loss. While none of us want to die, small adjustments to how we live our lives, who we discuss our possible but inevitable demise with and what provision or considerations we, at minimum, voice to close family or loyal friends, will ease the path of those who may have to deal with sudden or unexpected death.

- Islay remembers Nancy (to whom this book is dedicated) who died of cancer in 2014. In her final days in the St. Richard's Hospice, Worcester, we were allowed to bring her Pyrenean Mountain Dog (a very large breed) into the hospice to see her. Even in her final days, her face would light up when she saw her dog and some very special warm moments were shared between the two. Without doubt that contact eased the pain, physically and emotionally of Nancy's final days.
- Horses (among other animals) are now recognised as being vital in the role of support and empathy with people suffering from dementia,

bereavement and a range of other conditions that disrupt the mental wellbeing of the sufferer. Their quiet gentleness, in an atmosphere of sadness and impending loss of a life, can ease those present into a calm state of peace and acceptance to softly move to an inevitable outcome. (X.Ref Ch 11. Pammy and Islay)

Rehabilitation of Offenders:
Some 'children' (under the age of adulthood – 18 years) may for a variety of reasons find themselves struggling in mainstream life and education. They may have been excluded from school, struggle to maintain a secure and supportive home life and exist in a circumstance between families in foster care or social care. From this precarious situation they can descend, through no fault of their own and all too frequently, into any of the conditions that we have already touched on.

Many local authorities are recognising the role the horse can play in rehabilitating offenders and give them a future in life.

Eva Hamilton from 'Key4Life'.
During the lockdown for 'Covid 19' Islay put the time to good use by having some fascinating conversations with some amazing people who were willing to share their expertise and experiences with us for the benefit of 'Horses for Life'. The following discourse was between Islay and Eva Hamilton. This remarkable lady has been a pioneer for those disadvantaged by life and disadvantaged in society. Her vision, drive and passion were palpable, even over the phone. Her contribution to those less fortunate, involving her love of horses, is outlined here. I hope you will find it as inspiring, as I did, speaking to her.

Q: What is your involvement with horses?
A: I grew up in County Wicklow in Ireland and at an early age horses became my 'place to go' for stability, as sometimes there were challenges to my confidence and safety at 'home'.

In spite of this I grew up in a privileged childhood where Pony Club, hunting and a pony called 'Duke' were a huge part of my early life.

By my late teens I had been in several schools and was not clear in what I wanted to do with my life.

At the age of 18 I travelled to India and worked in the Mother Theresa's home for the dying. Here I experienced 'a calling' where I knew that my purpose in life was to 'serve' others.

Horses have always been my passion and I have always had horses in my life, although I spent many years in London where my access to horses on a regular basis was more limited.

Q: How did your charitable work start?

A: I was in the right place at the right time and met HRH Prince Charles while working for a lady called Dame Julia Cleverdon, who was running one of the Prince's charities.

HRH came up with the idea of creating a charity called 'Seeing is Believing' which I ran for him for around five years. The concept was to take business leaders into the inner cities of Britain to help develop disadvantaged, disaffected communities and reduce homelessness.

From that I set up 'Ready for Work', which was a model for homeless people to get them into employment.

During this time, I kept a horse outside London at Chessington. His name was 'Warrior' and he was Irish. It was impossible to mount him from the ground (he was regarded as dangerous and perhaps if we had not found each other his future would have been limited) but he became my best friend and my 'go to' safe place when I was low.

After some twenty years I moved to Somerset and was able to indulge my passion with horses again more fully.

My next calling was to set up 'The Warrior Programme' for ex-servicemen and women returning from duty in war torn countries, often with PTSD and other stresses borne from their experiences. I studied Neuro Linguistic Programming as a means to identify and unlock pain. I spent six years establishing a model that helped some 500 personnel 'get their lives back'.

Q: How did you get into work with young offenders?

A: In 2011, experiencing a personal 'wobble' in my life and seeing the London riots where some very young children were 'on the streets', I decided I had to do something about the youngsters who were at risk of ending up in prison, or who were already in prison.

In 2012 I set up 'Skills4life', a programme in three parts:

1. Unlocking pain from the past.
2. Employability – Preparing for work.
3. Ongoing support.

The use of horses in this initiative has been absolutely phenomenal in changing tough young men, who were already in prison or well on the path to ending up in prison.

I took horses into Ashfield Prison, then a Young Offenders prison. I was warned that it housed some extremely tough and aggressive young men from 15 to 18 years old. My first visit was pretty frightening, I walked into an environment with 23 young men who had absolutely no respect for me as a person, and especially as a woman. Then we brought in our horses. Many of these young men had never seen a horse close to before, maybe they had seen one on TV but never in the flesh. They were visibly frightened by the size of the horses and this showed their vulnerability.

That first occasion I had brought in two mares and the horses showed tension and anxiety because of the 'atmosphere of fear'. As the young men allowed themselves to 'find out about the horses' the fear dissipated and the horses began to show a connection with them. Ears back and tension then eased to become quiet breathing (from horse and inmate)

As the horses 'let them in' the transformation in atmosphere, relaxation and empathy was palpable and beautiful.

The inmates had to 'look at themselves' – 'consider the unresolved anger that was holding them back' – consider the fear, guilt or both, that they carried as a burden to limit their ability to move on with their lives.

Over time with the access to the horses they learnt to work together with the horses and each other. Some took a 'leap of faith' and with trust (a resource never experienced before) they would get on a horse to learn to ride.

I worked with young prisoners and with youngsters who were at risk of going to prison. As soon as they 'shift their energy' they then learn to think positively and can gradually move out of the cycle of depression that has a downward spiral.

We try to place them into the type of environment where they can thrive. Some go into racing yards, some into Polo. When released from prison we work with the probation service to find them work placements.

Many were re-offenders, who were not necessarily going into their favourite job, but we try to place the personality in the right type of situation. Drug dealers need to have a 'big bold job'. Followers are the easiest to deal with. Some juveniles have had no parental control ever and many have been in the care system with little future direction. Many will have been involved with knife crime.

All these disturbed individuals will work with horses and the horses have the most amazing influence over them because the horses are non-judgemental.

Q: What has been your greatest challenge?

A: Overcoming a system, I then suffered personal burnout and had to address my own potential breakdown by confronting my own pain. I have two amazing children, a son and daughter who I am so proud of. I love my charities, but I have to recognise that they must not overwhelm me. I have learnt to see that although there have been times when I thought I was being drawn away from something, I then realised that through that, I was being directed to something better.

Q: Describe yourself in three words.

A: Passionate - Driven -Spiritual. I want to make a difference. I want to help people.

Q: Do you have a favourite quote?

A: 'Yesterday is gone. Tomorrow has yet to come. We only have today – let us begin."

§

Reflections:

- Life in the 21st century can be highly pressurised with bombardment from all directions. Pace of life, pressures of school, work, relationships with significant others, not to mention social media and technological influences, are all contributors.

- Every generation will have managed its own pressures and circumstances. One only has to read a history book to be able to consider what life was like in the early part of the 20th century.

- Consider World War 1, when our beloved horses were requisitioned to fight the war. If you have not read Michael Morpurgo's 'War Horse', seen the stage play, or film, then you have missed a vital part of your 'horse empathy education'!

- During the World War 2 years, severe food rationing, fear of invasion, work force depleted due to conscription, etc. hugely influenced life and the future.

- Managing current life circumstances for ourselves and our nearest and dearest, can become a major consideration if we personally, or any of those significant others, are affected by any of the subjects discussed in this Chapter.

- Seek advice and support if necessary or skilled professional help if required.

- 'No man is an island.' Support from whichever direction is available is essential. Support from a liaison with horses can prove the vital key to help turn a person's life around and give them a more positive future.

Summary:
- This chapter has highlighted so many situations where adults and youngsters can find themselves in a downward spiral of negative circumstances.
- The horse can be the common denominator in serving those disadvantaged through life's dealing hand, and become the life saving factor to bring a damaged life back on track to a brighter future.
- There are many cross references to information in other chapters, proving convincingly that the 'horse is for life'. For those of us who are fortunate to share our lives with this wonderful creature, we are able to grow, thrive, recover or rehabilitate in so many ways by sharing the horse's non-judgemental empathy and innate strength to support us.
- Horses can, and will, help you to thrive again whatever your circumstances.

CHAPTER NINE

MANAGING THE 'PACE OF LIFE':

KEY POINTS:
- Work/life balance
- Marriage/Family
- Rest/time out and away

- Down time/ 'Me time'
- Complementary activities
- Sharing horses with 'significant others'.

Work/Life balance:

This is a subject that is well exposed, discussed, dictated and debated over, in today's busy life. Most weekend publications, monthly magazines and radio/television programmes regularly bring it up as a subject for an article or 'celebrity opinion' on how best to manage it.

The main consideration for us in the horse industry is that 'the horse' cannot be fitted into a 38 hour week! The reality of having a horse, or more often than not, more than one horse, in our lives means a 24/7 commitment, 365 days of the year. Horses have no conception of 'Christmas Day', long summer holidays or a day off because you decide to 'have a day off work'! Horses need your commitment to them, in the same way that you expect them to 'perform' with consistency when you ride or compete at that all important competition. If you decide to take 'a random day off', then horses suffer and/or your work colleagues have an unexpected and unwelcome increase in their workload. That 'random day off' is frequently on a cold

winter's morning or a wet, blustery day when you wake up early, hear the weather and would rather stay in bed! It has happened to us all countless times, but that moment when you decide to 'pull a sicky' is the moment when you let the horses you love, your colleagues you work with as a team and yourself down. The simple answer to preventing that from happening, is the moment you awake or hear the alarm go off, you 'in that moment' get out of bed!

As your feet hit the floor, take one or two deep breaths and be grateful that you are fortunate enough to be going out to 'be with horses'.

Significant Others

Before proceeding further in this chapter, let us clarify '**significant others**'! In every horsey environment there will be one or more members of the family/group/business/competition yard, etc, who are the 'die hard' individuals committed to the horse, come what may, irrespective of any other consideration.

Then there will be the members of that group who have, through no fault of their own, either as a partner, owner, friend, relative or other random reason, become 'attached' to the horsey fanatic! These magnanimous souls, mostly having saintly characteristics, are the wonderful supportive band of worthy people that this chapter will refer to as '**significant others**'.

CASE STUDY:

Many years ago, Cynthia and Tabitha (both completely fanatical 'horse people') were at a party with their respective partners.

Cynthia had already been married to her long-suffering husband, who had gone through the stages of learning to ride, owning a horse for a brief time, helping Cynthia at shows and writing for her when she judged Dressage. He had since moved into the state of 'you do your thing with horses' and I'll follow Rugby, dog walk, garden and holidays (when you can spare the time) and the occasional weekend away together. The equilibrium between the couple was generally secure and agreed.

Tabitha was newly engaged and at the party Cynthia overheard the following conversation between the two guys. Tabitha's partner asked, "How do you put up with these damned horses?". Cynthia's partner immediately replied very benignly, and in a matter of fact way, "Oh you get used to it!". Tabitha's partner snarled back, "well I won't". Cynthia remembers being shocked and saddened at what she regarded as a 'bad omen' to the impending partnership. Making no further reference to what she had overheard, the marriage took place and time elapsed. The 'omen' was self-fulfilling, the marriage lasted less than five years. Tabitha's husband was never prepared to share his wife with 'the damned horses', he made her choose, and she didn't choose him!

Marriage and family:

The authors of this book are blessed (we think!), to have two of the most long-suffering and supportive husbands on this planet.

Brian (Hutton), himself a senior, skilled, and much valued Instructor, has an active partnership with Pammy in Talland School of Equitation, the family business.

David (Auty) has known Islay since she was a 16 year old school girl, obsessed with horses, and has always supported her in her passion for the horse. Islay's Father, at their wedding, stated: "I admire my new son-in-law, not only has he taken on my daughter but also her horses"!

The long and short of it is that 'horses for life' mean horses in your life, come 'hell or high water' and so 'significant others' have to accept that, to coin a well known phrase, 'there will be three (or more) in the relationship!'

So how can we (the horse obsessed individual) take some responsibility for maintaining that all important equilibrium? To keep life in perspective is really hard and needs commitment. Getting the balance right between being dedicated and yet having time in life for other things, is not at all easy.

- 'It is not until you have lost someone or something very precious that the whole world stops and changes for ever'.
- 'No one wants to die but that inevitability is a certainty'.
- 'Every moment is precious' and 'we are only here once'.

All these statements are easily tripped off the tongue, but harder to carry out. Some of the case studies throughout this book should encourage us to 'take time' and learn to 'live in the moment'.

Both authors have suffered very close losses of a child and/or a sibling and have lived ever since with the huge hole that an unexpected loss imposes.

It is usually a natural progression of life that our parents will predecease us, however when you lose a sibling (especially an only sibling) you lose your childhood and the memories that you could only share with a sibling with whom you had grown up.

When you lose a child that is possibly one of the cruellest losses of all to have to live with. The hole is always there, it never goes away, you just learns to walk around it instead of continually falling into it. One learns to treasure the memory of the life lost, adjust to the future, without that special person. There is no option.

There should be a huge obligation to honour the memory of the lost loved one, by living life to the full as one rarely knows exactly when 'our clock will stop ticking'. It affects you for the rest of your life and should dictate how you allow time out from horses and other commitments, to include the very special 'significant others' who share our lives.

The involvement that so many of us have with the horse – **Horses for life**- is not just a sport or our industry, for us it is **"an art, a passion and a culture."**

Rest/Time Out and Away/Down Time/'Me Time':
Getting the balance right between being dedicated and yet having time in life for other things is not at all easy.

One of the ground rules from childhood upwards should be good bedtime habits, 'not burning the midnight oil', 'early to bed, early to rise makes a man healthy, wealthy and wise', these 'old sayings' hold their own wisdom.

Rest is fundamental to your health and well being. (X.ref Ch 6). Building regular and quality rest time into a work schedule is a valuable commodity to add as 'good practice'.

Islay spent seven months with Mrs Janet Sturrock FBHS while training for her BHSI (x Ref. Author profiles). Every day after a short lunch break, Mrs Sturrock went upstairs and lay on her bed for 20minutes. That period of time was absolutely 'non negotiable'! Everyone knew that she must never be disturbed during that time under any circumstances (unless her beloved horses were at risk!). She would say that in that 20mins she could 'cat nap',
wake refreshed and never get into a deeper sleep from which it was more difficult to rouse.

How one personally develops the ability to 'switch off' from the rigours of the day is an important skill to be able to develop. As with any other skill, it just needs practice! Being able to 'zone out' from one's surroundings for a short period of 'me time' is a powerful tool to be able to implement.

Sometimes music can help and these days there are any number of systems that allow you to manage 'your own personal playlist'. Headphones to enable you to 'be in your own place' may show a detached and uninvolved 'you', but if it helps you switch off and enjoy some 'me time', then it may be valuable.

Islay can sleep 'anywhere', waiting in busy airport departure lounges, on a plane before take-off, in a strange environment or any hotel bed! Often one hears, "I don't sleep well when I'm away from home". If that is frequently, then that is a disadvantage. If you are aiming for a restful holiday, not being able to sleep is a huge disadvantage to the benefits of the break. If you are on a tight schedule for work (attending a conference or giving a clinic) and your sleep is compromised, then your efficiency will also be inhibited. The health benefits of sleep are well documented, as are regimes to develop good sleep. Work at establishing a pattern that encourages you to sleep easily and soundly.

Tips to help develop a good sleep pattern:
- Learn to 'be in the moment', able to switch off from the worries of the day or the future and 'relax within that moment'. This will enable your body not to be in the constant state of 'anxiety' or 'flight mode'. (X Ref.Ch 6)
- 'Mindfulness', 'deep breathing' and 'meditation', all skills that can be 'acquired or learnt', facilitate a calmness especially in times of 'stress'. (X.ref. Ch8)
- Time off and away is valuable, especially if you are 'the boss'. Ensure that you have a structure 'at home' that you can leave in 'good hands', a structure that you trust and can walk away from without needing to call home to ensure there are no crises.
- That strong structure is probably one that you have established through sound training of your staff, developing a reliable workforce of individuals who are loyal to you, sharing your values and commitment. A work force that you have encouraged to show responsibility and 'manage' under your leadership. They then know you trust them and have belief in them, which is a valuable quality for their future and in building their self esteem.
- Remember, however, that they are not the Boss and therefore can never be expected to have the relentless commitment to working 24/7 that you inevitably do. (xRef Ch6 maintaining health and well being.)

Islay recalls advising a young person who was working for a well known rider some years ago. This 19 year old, was working a six day week with long hours and little time off, she also had to 'do her own horse' in her 'spare time' when her working day ended. Islay suggested to her that her employer was not recognising her youth, the need to have a balance in how hard she worked and what time off she needed. Her answer was "but they work so hard themselves, I can't expect more time when they don't have it themselves." Islay pointed out: "that is their choice and it is their business, so they are ultimately the beneficiaries". This was a case of total commitment from the rider but not recognising that in this situation the 'student' was a 'significant other' who, without due care from her employer would 'burn out' and choose another career.

Pammy says "to manage to stay married, find time for both 'children', teach to bring in an income, run a business, train and compete my own horses and to part-time write, sometimes has me (and those around me) in a spin – this is my ongoing challenge".

The authors are agreed that their teaching is their passion, often we can be exhausted after a long day's work, but our last lesson must be as committed and involved for the pupil as our first. We believe that, while there are many qualities a teacher should have, passion should be one of them. Pammy was once congratulated by a top trainer for 'teaching from the heart', following it with 'teaching like that you will wear yourself out'. We believe that no-one should teach without passion, caring and from the heart. Patience is always important, never giving up, but being patient is vital. Developing patience is definitely an ability that improves with age!

Complementary activities and 'sharing with significant others':
As we have discussed in Ch.2 horses may run in families.

Pammy has two prolifically competent children (Charlie and Pippa), who have ridden for GB in Junior and Young Rider Dressage Teams, and who are both now forging their own pathways as professionals in the horse industry. That vein does not always follow through the whole family.

Islay has one son (Robert), now married to Kate with two young sons of his own (James and Tom). Robert, in spite of growing up surrounded by his Mother's horses, under sufferance learning to ride, had no intention of following her into any type of equestrian career and followed his own passion, which has always been windsurfing and sailing.

The following suggestions may ensure a harmony between the 'horse fanatic' and the significant others. They must be worked at and fiercely respected, so that the significant other(s) does not feel that they always have to play 'second fiddle' to the 'damned horses'! (X.Ref case study Cynthia/Tabitha)

- Keep one day of the week horse free – a family day – where lunch or an evening meal is a family affair. Ideally this would be at a weekend (maybe Sunday) but this will need serious managing, as competitions inevitably fall on a Sunday and these might be relevant and important in the calendar of development.
- Planning well ahead is pivotal to good competition management anyway, so this can be scheduled well in advance on a quarterly or at least bimonthly planner.
- Sit down as a family, with the calendar or better still a year planner. Put in firm dates for holidays, short 'away breaks', free Sundays and alternatives if the family Sunday is a necessary competition date.
- If the family are split – one child doing one thing and one doing another, then parents must plan for one parent to go with one child and one with the other.
- Islay recollects a European Pony Dressage Championships in Germany with one sibling on the GB Team, while the other sibling was in Italy on the GB Young Rider European team. Now that took some planning, one parent with the Pony rider, and the other parent with the Young rider. Both teams won medals that year if Islay remembers correctly – thank goodness!
- Family time is sacrosanct (x.Ref. Profile of authors). It is a time for sharing, having fun, rejuvenating and resting. It is a time for making memories to last a lifetime.
- Be interested in the activities of your 'significant others'. Be prepared to go and watch them if they have a sporting passion, unless they are happy for you to do 'your thing with the horses' while they do theirs in another sphere. Make time to be involved with their interest.
- Islay knows a great deal about 'windsurfing'! The best aspect is that the board lives in the garage when you are not 'playing' with it. It does not need shoeing, veterinary care or any attention except when you securely fix it to the roof rack of the car! She knows it costs a minute amount of money compared to her co-author, who had to fund two children to ride, so all in all time spent watching her son indulge his passion on water, was an easy option for Islay.
- Islay's husband Bowls (Green Bowling) in the Summer. Do not let anyone

tell you that unless you are a Dressage fanatic, 'dressage is boring to watch' until you have watched Bowling! To sit (hopefully in the sun) on a warm afternoon with the excuse of watching Bowling is, however, a very calming and peaceful way to pass an afternoon!

- Pammy on the other hand had to manage her stress levels, in training and observing both her children through their developing competitive years. Both fiercely competitive and increasingly opinionated. Islay was often called in to sit with Pammy at the working in, to ensure that over anxiety of the parent to produce a winning performance, did not erupt into aggravation between parent and child, in their combined efforts to generate that winning outcome.

- When asking a young person at the start of their career with horses, what are their hobbies or other interests? If the answer is nothing, I only have time for horses, this can ring alarm bells.

- 'Switch off time' is vital for health and wellbeing. Whether it is meeting friends, reading, going to the gym or something completely different, regular time away from horses is good for you and it is good for the horse.

- It can be remarkable and fascinating to discover complementary activities that appeal to horsey fanatics and their significant others. These should be explored and developed, to ensure that the sharing of life is enhanced for the making of good memories and not overwhelmed by the extensive time stolen by 'horses for life'.

CASE STUDY:

Peter and Harriet had always shared a love of horses, both riding as children and then developing through Pony Club. They met as young adults while hunting and then socially through 'Young Farmers'.

They married and, while both following non horsey careers (Harriet working in the family business and Peter in horticulture), they established a small yard at home of half a dozen thoroughbred horses which were trained under permit, and Peter rode as a Point to Point rider. In due course a daughter, Sally, arrived and of course she started to ride. Pony Club, Showing and Pony Racing appealed to her. Speed, challenge and excitement suited the whole family as they skied regularly.

In time as Sally grew up, the racehorses were eased out and the yard started to fill with event horses. The gradual progression of this 'family love affair with the horse', has seen the racehorses eased into retirement, the increase of young and developing Event horses as Sally has progressed from pony rider to young adult. Peter and Harriet keep the horses at home, fit and managed. Sally fitted in training and competing around Boarding School, a gap year and then University.

The key to this family success is they share what they all do and they enjoy the family experience of planning (Harriet and Sally), managing the horses work, fitness, wellbeing (Peter/Harriet and Sally) and Sally competing. They all ride together frequently in the fittening work, they all hold an HGV licence (Heavy Goods Vehicle) so all can drive the lorry, they all commit to their various roles at competitions and have in general a wonderful family experience of 'horses for life'.

Reflections:

- Those of us who have 'horses in our lives' are challenging people to live with, because there has to be some sharing.
- It is manageable to have 'horses for life' but the challenge of sharing must be recognised and planned especially with 'significant others', who may need to learn to adapt.
- Horses in our lives can be a 'double edged sword', they should make us more caring/giving/empathetic, but sometimes they make us more selfish in not recognising the needs of 'significant others' in our lives too.
- See yourself as 'other people see you' and as a result, match up to sharing time and commitment with your loved ones.
- Good forward planning and communication with those 'significant others' will ensure a harmonious acceptance from all, of the role of the 'horse being in your life'.

Summary:

'Horses in our lives' for many of us, are a non-negotiable fact of life. For those wanting to share our lives closely, who come into a horsey environment but do not necessarily share or inherit that passion, there can be a feeling of alienation, or even jealousy, of the position the horse holds in the loved one's life. It is essential that this feeling is recognised, accepted and managed for the mutual benefit of all involved.

CHAPTER TEN

HORSES WITHOUT RIDING

KEY POINTS:
- **Volunteering**
- **Owning or sharing a competition horse**
- **Stewarding**
- **Unique interview**
- **Judging**
- **Keeping a retired horse or companion**
- **Watching/learning**
- **Yard visits**
- **Contact with horses**

Volunteering:

The Equestrian world would grind to a halt without volunteers. (X.Ref RDA Ch 8) Competitions especially, depend on the willingness, skill and experience of volunteers in countless roles. We will highlight a few in this chapter and also give a fascinating interview with a British Dressage and FEI Steward, who has travelled at home and internationally in his role as a 'volunteer'.

If you still want your 'fix' of seeing, smelling, patting, admiring or just being in the proximity of a horse, then any of the following roles could fulfil your needs.

Writing for a dressage judge:

At pure Dressage competitions or at Horse Trials (Events), a writer is often a much sought after volunteer. This could be from local unaffiliated competitions through Pony Club/Riding Club/affiliated competitions to Regional, National and International classes. It is a developing skill, but even in its simplest form, the fundamental requirement is, that you can listen to the commentary given by the judge as they watch the performance and write down on a score sheet their comments and marks. 'Writing' is a great way to learn more about the 'way of going' of a Dressage horse, the skill of the rider producing a reflection of their horse's training to the Judge, through a series of prescribed movements in the horse's three paces – walk/trot and canter. Most Dressage competition venues will be more than grateful to have a list of willing volunteers who are prepared to write for a dressage judge. It may be a couple of hours or depending on the length and importance of the competition, it could be half a day or more. In the case of International competitions, if you were allocated to an International judge it would involve four days of work.

Dressage, while sometimes being seen as the 'serious discipline' in the horse world, can nevertheless throw up some highly amusing incidents within a competition. Here is just a tiny taster of them, all experienced over Islay's lifetime being involved with dressage:

- You are judging and glance sideways to see that your writer has fallen asleep!

- You are judging an important Horse Trial selection class on a very windy day. Several of the selectors are parked in their cars behind your car at C. Suddenly, with a horse competing in front of you, a huge gust of wind causes four of the conical letter markers around the arena to take flight across the path of the startled horse and rider!

- You are writing for an elderly, highly respected judge. In the back of the car is the judge's ageing, rather obese, dribbly and smelly, but much-loved dog. Halfway through the competition, said dog decides that your lap would be a much more comfortable place to languish for the remainder of the class. You are learning much from the knowledge and experience of this renowned judge but the discomfort, increasing smells and flatulence emanating from this canine become a challenging 'price to pay'. You make a mental note that, when you become a more eminent Judge, you will never inflict this imposition on a young keen writer.

- You are judging a Horse Trial with five arenas packed quite closely together in a small flat field. You are in the arena nearest the entrance from the working in and are in the middle of judging a partnership, when a horse and rider randomly rides across your arena to get to another arena, totally oblivious to the fact that they are crossing an arena and disrupting someone's test! Fortunately, 'my' competitor was a professional and highly experienced International rider competing on a young horse. He completely disregarded the intruder and carried on as if nothing had happened. The intruder carried on towards the next arena, still unaware of the potential mayhem they could have caused!

- You arrive at a venue to judge an unaffiliated competition and drive into a field to find a pile of white arena boards and a set of markers waiting for someone (it turns out to be you) to first build the arena!

- You judge a horse trials for four hours, in appalling weather, with the rain lashing down. By the time you finish your car (Your husband's pride and joy, not a four by four) is marooned on a tiny patch of green grass where you parked at silly o'clock in the morning. All around you is like a ploughed field, where hundreds of horses have worked in and forty have ridden down the centreline towards you. In no way will your car even contemplate driving out! You wait another three hours to be towed out by the only tractor on site, which is busy towing lorries out on a different part of the property. You make a mental note to buy a four by four or never judge a horse trial in the rain on grass in your husband's car again!

- You set out on a bright sunny May morning to drive two hours to a prestigious Horse Trials venue in smart attire, as you know it will be a formal sponsors lunch with other 'important' judges. By the time you get there, the weather has broken, the sky is full of angry dark clouds, which deteriorate into a cold, wet day, and you have not taken an appropriate array of alternative clothing (how could you trust the weather forecast – you are British for heaven's sake!). You finish judging and then teeter to the hospitality in your 'strappy sandals' to sit making polite conversation, while you freeze to death with your co-judges, who have, of course, covered all eventualities!

- You are writing for an International Judge at C in a European U21 Championship, using hospitality new cars provided as advertising from a well-known brand of four by four vehicle. Your foreign judge accidentally leans on the door lock of the vehicle, which then causes the automatic car alarm to be activated and there is a horse in the arena. The vehicle's horn starts blaring, the other judges look concerned, the rider falters and then carries on riding the test. The Judge carries on judging and you keep writing. The horn stops - but only for thirty seconds - then it starts again. The rider then (not surprisingly), goes wrong and the Judge can't stop him because the horn is still blaring! The rider manages to make his own correction, the judge manages to open the door to silence the horn and the test is somehow completed. Mayhem ensues, as the other two judges come to the President and so does the chef d'equipe of the rider (from Poland). The Judge waves off the problem saying: "it is like an aircraft flying over, it is the luck of the competition". He refuses to re-judge the horse even though the other two judges are requesting this. After a break, and further discussion, the decision is made that the horse will be re-judged at the end of the class. To everyone's amazement the chef d'equipe returns soon after to say "no the rider is happy with his mark (from the disastrous performance), he has the best score he has had on the horse and does not wish to be rejudged!"

- Yes, writing is a fun alternative in which to get involved and may create some fascinating and amusing experiences.

All disciplines have their own system of 'trained professional Stewards' (see the interview later in this chapter). All competitions from unaffiliated upwards through Pony Club, Riding Club to the higher levels of structured competitions need stewards.

A steward's role may cover any of the following:
- Organising parking.
- Organising entry (through ticket control)
- Organising seating.
- Managing welfare, health and safety of anyone on site.
- Being prepared for any kind of emergency (possibly requiring evacuation of a venue)
- Managing the competitor order for dressage/show jumping/cross country.

The following may be an over generalisation, for which we offer an apology, but is more often than not reflecting of the authors' experience.

Anyone with any past experience of competition with horses, will know that the 'dressage fraternity' tend to be more polite, biddable and will generally abide by the 'rules'.

Eventers (because they do dressage as well as event) will tend to be fairly biddable, if they consider a request to be fair and reasonable.

Show jumpers may well prove to be a 'law unto themselves' and require a highly organised and firm steward, to control a running order of competition, which more often than not is allocated only on whose number is written on a blackboard at the entrance to the competition arena.

The latter requires a loud voice and a strong resolve, to prevent the 'I've got four horses to jump so I have to jump one NOW rider' from monopolising the running order and pushing in to a list of riders who have dutifully been trying to adhere to some system of courtesy to fellow competitors. Inevitably there is usually at least one rider who will attempt to intimidate the long-suffering steward with the question "don't you know who I am?" to which an experienced Steward will swiftly reply on one of the following lines:-

"should that make any difference?", "oh I am sorry, have you forgotten your identity?" or "I'm afraid today it is the same for everyone"!

Standing up for oneself early on, ensures that the word gets around that the 'rules' must be adhered to and the Steward is in charge. Of course, competitors are 'stressed' and 'revved up' but there is no excuse for lack of courtesy to the wonderful volunteers that keep our activities with horses possible. (X Ref. RDA)

As Covid 19 lockdown has progressed, it has certainly assisted in the progress of this book but the interviews that the authors set up have largely had to be conducted either on the phone or by e.mail.

Geoff Simpson: British Dressage & FEI International Steward

Geoff Simpson is a well-known British Dressage and FEI international Steward. His account of personal development towards his stewarding role, on retirement as a Deputy Head Teacher, makes great reading and is an insight into the sensitivity, adaptability, tact and diplomacy needed to be a conduit towards helping competitors achieve their best in competition.

Q: Who or what got you started in stewarding?

A: My wife and I came to the Midlands in the early 1970s. One day we visited a Pony Club event and my wife bumped into someone she had known in her teenage years when she had her own pony. We were asked if we could help at Hagley Hall Horse Trials with the Dressage. After a little questioning as to what was involved, we said yes and helped steward the single section on the Friday afternoon, not really knowing what we were to do until we got there. During the break in the class someone appeared from the house with tea, served on a tray, china cups and cake. We thought we could do this – it never happened again!

However, our cards were marked, and we went to other trials deeper into Worcestershire, where we met Janet Plant (now well-known BE Course Designer and organiser of major horse trials), who asked us if we would run the Dressage at the Horse Trials at Weston Park. Approximately 10 years later we gave this up as it was very time consuming, having grown into a twice yearly, world renowned, International Event, covering classes from novice to advanced over four days .

In about 2002 I met Chris Porterfield (BD Judge, International Para Judge and Steward) at the British Dressage Winter Championships at Solihull Riding Club. Not having a great deal to do, as my wife was writing for a Dressage Judge, I helped Chris with some of the more mundane things in the stewarding area. As is often the case one cannot escape once involved, and it progressed from there.

Q: What specific skills or knowledge did you need?

A: At first it was very much an ability to communicate with people and having a rudimentary knowledge of horses and their various bits and saddlery. The latter came very rapidly as fortunately I did have time to learn, as by then I was retired from my profession.

Q: Your profession was as a teacher. What attributes were transferable into your stewarding role?

A: I had had a very senior role in the largest secondary school in the country and as such had to deal with children from 11 to 18+, as well as adults involved in a wide range of jobs in the school, together with parents and outside agencies. This meant that I had to be able to switch, often rapidly, from one situation to another, whilst remaining focused and calm. I am sure that this has helped me in several ways throughout my time stewarding.

Q: How long did it take before you were "qualified" to steward alone?

A: I think it was about 18 months. In those days, the early 2000s, the training was not as structured as it is now and there were not as many stewards.

Q: What pleasure or satisfaction do you get from stewarding?

A: It gives me great pleasure being able to help people, hopefully, achieve their hopes and ambitions. This applies at all levels, whether at a World Championship, Olympic Games, British Regional and National Championships, or Youth competitions. It is important that they have achieved their best at their level, and they all deserve the same kind of respect and help in whatever way possible. I have met many people from all walks of life, and I like to think I have become friends with many of them. It is good to be appreciated, and I think respected, as a Steward. The words that are used to describe stewarding are: "Help – Prevent – Intervene" and rarely have I had to use all three following each other. I remember from my days in teaching that an appropriate look can save a thousand words. I try to bring this into my work. I also get satisfaction in being able to help in maintaining the welfare of the horses in all ways whilst at competitions.

Q: Where has stewarding taken you? (practically, travel wise and emotionally – personal experience?)

A: Nationally, stewarding has taken me all over Britain (Northern Ireland being the only exception to this), and given me opportunities to visit places which perhaps I would not have seen. I was fortunate to work at the World Games in Kentucky, USA 2010, and of course London 2012. I have had 3 other invitations to work abroad, none of which have actually come to fruition yet. Once to Italy but I was already committed to a National Competition in the UK, and secondly, to Norway, but I was on holiday in Norway at the time, "Would my wife miss me for a few days?" I asked with a tongue in cheek, and finally for Tokyo 2020 (hopefully next year) but maybe I am jinxed.

What about emotionally? Well, I was fortunate enough to be based on the field of play when GB won their Gold medal at London 2012, and I tack checked all of the four British horses. This had been a prior agreement between me and my colleague to do alternate horses, before the running order was published. At British competitions, the Regional and National Championships are for those competitors who have qualified for 'their Olympic Games' and it means such a lot to them, especially the first time they achieve this goal. However, many of them are so extremely nervous, whether they are children or others perhaps past their youth. I feel I have provided a service above and beyond the basic stewarding if I can make them feel relaxed and help them to perform at their best. It is always good to see competitors finish with a smile on their face. I am not happy when riders immediately blame their horse, "A poor workman always blames his tools".

Q: What has been your worst experience and why?

A: Being abused publicly by an organiser. No further comment!

Q: Most amusing experience?

A: Last year a lady asked me if her number was 'two, six, nought' or 'two hundred and sixty'! Not being "lost for words", I was for a moment or two. So, I checked her saddle cloth and sure enough the digits were in the correct order. "One moment" I said, "I will check my running order – what would you prefer it to be?". "Two hundred and sixty" was the reply. "Well that's good", said I, "that's what you have". Off she went to warm up, another satisfied customer. I did allow myself a smile.

Q: Most rewarding experience?

A: It must be London 2012 I suppose. However, when competitors come back to see me to say they have won, usually with a great smile, that is extremely rewarding. After being involved with British Dressage Under 25 Championships at Sheepgate Equestrian for a number of years now, it is rewarding to watch these young people grow up and develop over the years and eventually become international riders – I suppose that is the teacher in me!

Q: Describe yourself in three words.

A: (From my wife in the British Dressage Magazine) - Kind, sympathetic and reliable. "I'll take those!!"

Q: Do you have a favourite quote?

A: Not really but I do like "You can take a horse to water but you can't make it drink", perhaps appropriate in view of my present situation.

Owning or sharing a competition horse.

Owning or sharing in the costs of a competition horse(s) can be a hugely rewarding experience. It is a well-known practice in Racing, where a 'syndicate' of people may share the initial purchase of the horse and then contribute to the 'running costs' of the horse.

The cost may be a substantial contribution (depending on the number in the syndicate, which could vary from a small group of under five or maybe into the tens, twenties or more). Inevitably the ongoing regular outgoings of full livery, shoeing, veterinary, entries and travel costs can develop into a large monthly commitment.

Rarely will the winnings of your racehorse match the ongoing regular outgoings, however the interest of 'following your horse' in his training and racing, the camaraderie of sharing with other likeminded owners and travelling around the country to watch your horse 'run' outweighs the cost, if you can afford it.

A similar 'ownership' part or full, can be possible with a competition horse in any of the three Olympic disciplines. If your interest is with one particular discipline, it can be immense fun to travel the country watching 'your horse(s)' compete. Again you meet likeminded people at competitions around your area, or even farther afield, and become 'one of the crowd' relating to the specific horse, receiving relevant passes to the bigger competitions where your horse may be competing.

You can be involved as much, or as little, as you choose but developing a good working relationship with your rider is essential. They should value you greatly as a benefactor and not underestimate your support and generosity.

The working relationship between a rider and an owner is vitally important to both parties and reliant on a clear and open understanding, which should be in writing for the benefit of both. Regular scheduled meetings should be part of the ongoing liaison between rider and owner, to ensure that both are well informed of current circumstances (e.g. ground goes hard, so rider withdraws from an intended event due to the 'going' not suiting the horse. Owner is going away for a month and would prefer that the horse does not compete during their absence).

Clear guidelines should be in place to manage a situation of the potential sale of a horse that you own, that a rider has taken up through the levels. The horse may have become extremely valuable and there is often an optimum time to sell. There must be a clear division of funds between owner and rider, which ideally should be pre-established, before the temptation of mega bucks being offered muddies the water of clarity, cooperation and understanding between you and your rider.

Your rider should respect your input (other than just for paying the bills), not expect you to be a constant 'cash machine' for whatever new piece of equipment that may take their fancy. Many riders benefit hugely from relationships that have lasted years, become firm friendships and provided successive horses for a rider to compete.

Keeping a retired horse or a companion:
Often if you have owned a competition horse then, when he is coming to the time that he will retire from competition, you may have him 'home' to see out his older years in the peace and security of a 'retirement environment'.

Some horses may still be capable of providing good education, either at a lower level of competition, in the hunting field or hacking. You may have a young relative or friend who would love the opportunity to ride this ex-competition horse.

Horses in their twenties can provide companionship and be a 'nanny' to a younger horse(s). It is of course vital that any horse in retirement is regularly checked for overall wellbeing, that diet is appropriate to prevent the horse becoming overweight or underweight, teeth are checked once or twice a year, and feet and worming programmes maintained.

Remember that horses are herd animals and thrive in company. It is rare that a horse living alone is 'a happy horse'.

Welfare organisations such as 'World Horse Welfare' and Red Wings

Horse Sanctuary' among others, are always looking for knowledgeable, caring homes where an older, or previously neglected, horse can live out his retirement years in peace and wellbeing. These organisations will always 'approve' a new owner before rehoming a horse with you and then remain as a 'go to' support should your circumstances change, and you are no longer able to sustain the horse's welfare.

Judging:
Earlier in this chapter there is reference to 'writing for a Dressage Judge'.
- If you have had an active and involved life with horses, then there may be a clear avenue for you to judge (in your chosen discipline – if for some reason you are no longer able or fit to ride)
- Judging (Show horses, Dressage, Show Jumping or scoring at a Horse Trials) requires a secure, confident, technical knowledge of the discipline.
- It requires a passion to want to 'put back into the sport' to give other riders a knowledgeable and unbiased opinion of a 'performance'. Marks or scores should be awarded by the Judge to the rider for their commitment to produce a performance matching, as near as possible, the 'blueprint of correctness' expected at the level of competition being assessed.
- A Show Jumping Judge is only required to score, in compliance with the BS Rules, whether a rider jumps all the fences on the course, in the correct order, going through the start and finish, whether clear, lowers a number of poles, has a refusal, fall or misses a fence, within the time allowed. This type of judging is easily recognised as being objective.
- However, the Judges must also ensure the rider is on the correct horse shown on the start list. It is also their responsibility to ensure the rider's dress and horse's tack meet the rules for the competition, and that the horse is not mistreated by inappropriate use of whip, spurs or bit. The Senior Judge is also responsible for ensuring the fences are built to the rules of the competition. There are usually two Judges, who are required to communicate with the collecting ring, record each fence jumped, both on a computer to comply with the British Showjumping (BS) App and a written sheet (they do not often have a writer), manage the time clock, recording times to achieve results, often commentate, and at the same time observe the competitor jump each fence. A Show Jumping Judge's box is generally not as calm as Dressage judging.
- Judging Dressage is challenging in a different way, as the judge must assess a test movement by movement, against the 'objective criteria' of the scales

of training of the horse and the effect and influence of the rider's position and aids. Not only does this take skill, timing and concentration (no chance of a quick 'instant replay' to see that movement again because you sneezed and missed it!) but a mark must be given swiftly, leaving personal bias aside (you don't like Arabs, can't stand cobs or coloured horses, you think the latter look like cows!).

- Judging Dressage can be very satisfying and keeps you involved in a very worthwhile way.
- Judging Show classes may also be an avenue open to you, if you have had involvement and experience in the world of showing horses. Starting with unaffiliated classes and working with a more experienced judge(s) is the way to gather more knowledge and experience to consolidate your own expertise and gradually move up the ranks.

Yard visits

Many top riders now offer yard visits at their establishments on a regular basis. These visits may be organised through your local Riding club or Pony Club but may also be advertised on the website of the relevant rider. Visits will vary from rider to rider but will usually include:

- Watching the training of horses from young horses to advanced.
- Watching the training of younger apprentices or members of staff.
- Being able to question about training methods
- A tour of the yard facilities.
- A meeting with some of the 'celebrity horses' who may be current or past top competition horses.
- Seeing 'household names' like Carl Hester, Valegro and Charlotte DuJardin (Olympic Gold medallists from London 2012 and Rio 2016) up close and in person can be a memorable, once in a lifetime, experience never to be forgotten, making memories for life.

If you need to have a 'regular fix' of seeing, feeling, smelling horses, then there are ways and means wherever you are in this country or abroad. Fortunately, horses are fairly easy to find wherever you are in city or country.

Islay recalls one occasion when she had been in London for a few days and was feeling starved of a 'horse fix'. Walking down towards Horse Guards Parade in Central London on a cold, wet day, Islay saw a Guardsman mounted on a horse doing Sentry duty at the entrance to Horseguards. Her husband was horrified when Islay just had to cross the road to 'pat the horse'!

Her justification was that she had not seen a horse for days. The Guardsman, no doubt had seen it all before but maintained his totally imperious persona, making no acknowledgement of this mad woman crossing the road to chat to his horse!

Reflections:

- There are many ways that you can still immerse yourself in the 'love of the horse'. Some can be costly (owning a competition horse) but many only need a commitment of time, and maybe some ongoing learning.
- There is much learning to be achieved in volunteering, watching and listening.
- Being involved with horses can assist in an individual's personal well being, stave off loneliness and give one a sense of being needed – not only by the horse but by other like-minded individuals.

Summary:

- We are coming to the end of our mission.
- We hope you have gained some inspiration, motivation, drive and determination from some or all of what you have read.
- We hope our passion emanates from every chapter, and that you too can either understand or share that feeling, or realise that it is never too late to find your love of the horse.

CHAPTER ELEVEN

KICKING OVER THE TRACES.-THE FUTURE:

KEY POINTS:
- 'Reinventing the wheel' Ian Woodhead – pony dressage record.
- Future scoring of Dressage.
- What we have learnt and must remember.

- Riding Schools in 2020.
- Covid 19.
- Reminiscing and looking into the future
- Leaving unanswered questions
- There will always be horses
- 'Ode to the Horse'.

As a competitive nation in the three Olympic Disciplines: Dressage, Show Jumping and Eventing, GB has been at the forefront of all three since the Second World War. The fluctuations of success in each however, can be researched fairly easily, so we will not catalogue them here.

Dressage in Senior competition was definitely the 'poor relation' to the stronger European nations of Germany, Holland, Denmark and Sweden until the beginning of the 21st century, when the 'Carl Hester' influence began to bring Dressage from GB into the ascendency in Europe, and then worldwide. (X.Ref Ch3)

Eventing and Show Jumping have always maintained their strength in International competition.

Eventing - particularly a British strength, has flourished under the long-term national trainer Yogi (Goran) Breisner and then Chris Bartle.

Show Jumping has also had its 'purple patches', Olympic Team Gold at the London Olympics 2012 and Individual Gold for Nick Skelton at Rio Olympics 2016), with long-term team trainers Rob Hoekstra, followed by Di Lampard.

Let us consider the development of these disciplines through children, because surely it is from here that our future Olympians are spawned? Internationally children can compete on ponies (max height 14.2hh / 148cm) from the year of their 12th birthday to the year in which they attain the age of 16years. In Eventing and Show Jumping the pony results are outstanding.

Both disciplines have won countless team and individual medals since the inception of 'Pony European Championships' in 1977. The first Championships were held in Helsingborg, Sweden, which was a competition for Show Jumping and Dressage only, where seven teams from a variety of

European nations took part. Islay was chef d'equipe to the Dressage team and Fergus Graham was in charge of the Show Jumping team. Islay remembers that the Dressage team came last in every class and the Show Jumpers won every class. There was a combined prize for the team with the best overall result and the Brits won this on the strength of how well the Show Jumpers' had done, and definitely in spite of the Dressage contribution!

This lack lustre record of British Pony Dressage persisted into the late 1990s when a trainer called Ian Woodhead decided that here was a golden opportunity to develop the increasing interest that children were having in Dressage. As the overall interest in Dressage as a specialism was expanding, Ian pioneered a structure of developing interested young children riding ponies that would be specifically targeted for Dressage. He sourced ponies from Europe and either sold to the rider or maintained part ownership. Ian found many ponies (X Ref. Manitu N/Gigolo Ch4), often ridden and schooled by his own two talented daughters (both now International riders in their own right – Amy in Dressage and Holly in Eventing). Ian was appointed Trainer for the British Pony Dressage Squad and many riders went on to represent GB at pony level. From his base in Grimsby Yorkshire, he ran training weekends and was one of a pivotal number of forward-thinking people, in the establishment of the BYRDS (British Young Rider Dressage) Scheme. BYRDS (now BD Youth) also developed a series of winter training weekends, to identify and train potential youngsters interested in the early specialisation into Dressage.

From 1998 the British Pony Dressage Team competed in European Championships with increasing and consistent success. Between 1997 (UK - Hartpury) and 2005 (Italy - Pratoni) GB won nine consecutive medals, 7 Bronze and 2 Silver. The dominance of the German team at this level was overwhelming, with some competition in the top four teams of Denmark, Holland and Great Britain. During much of this time (2000 to 2006) Islay was chef d'equipe to the Pony team, with team Selectors the late Maureen Newall and Rachel Hillier, both highly respected National Judges, completing an administrative 'team' that worked tirelessly for the good of the riders and the success of each team. Maybe there are lessons to be learned from the cohesion that this group achieved, with this reflected in the consistency of results year on year for nearly a decade. There were a brief few golden years between 2012 and 2015 when international dressage judge/trainer/rider Peter Storr trained the British pony team with his protégé Phoebe Peters, who won team gold and five individual European medals.

Scoring dressage

One of the ongoing arguments around the sport of Dressage is that the scoring method is potentially subjective and open to personal or nationalistic bias. Other similarly scored sports such as Gymnastics and Ice Skating have moved towards a specific judging scheme designed around a code of points for each movement. Marks based on an 'excellent 10' could then be deducted relative to faults observed.

Wayne Channon, as Chair of the International Dressage Riders' Club (IDRC), has pioneered the concept of breaking everything down into components, then with a code of marks judges can break down the points they give accordingly. If the marking can be more systemised, then judges will be more consistent and help riders make calculated decisions in the arena. This concept has been, and continues to be, widely discussed and debated between top riders, trainers and judges both at home and abroad. It is currently being considered by a working group from the FEI (Federation Equestre Internationale)

What we have learnt and what we must remember

- When we have an all absorbing passion for our work, very little time is left over for family and friends. It seems that each decade passes more quickly, and the pace of life becomes faster. Becoming nearly 70 makes us think of what might have been, and, makes us more determined at what else we want to achieve before we die. All we have to offer is knowledge and experience, and sometimes that is based on 'what not to do'. It is so important that we get our mindset right. Positive, reactive, open, honest, kind and considerate, all qualities that we hope we share. It is an ongoing quest in life to gain insight, self awareness and achieve self improvement. Self criticism is also a requirement.

- Islay's favourite and much used statement is "Oh to see yourself as other people see you". It may well be a saying that applies equally to both authors! How you imagine yourself is not necessarily how other people (who don't know you) see you.

- (illustration – seeing yourself in the mirror or maybe something different?) No 43

- Pammy's self-appraisal would include, "humility, lack of tact could be improved, and a more smiling communication", she says, "less 'bark' and a better ability to listen".

- Islay would say "more tolerance with her husband – poor man! Probably also 'less bark', more patience and less need for everything to happen 'now'."

- Pammy's loss of her first daughter, Francesca, through 'cot death' has irrevocably changed her perspective on life:

Pammy's account: *"The greatest gift she gave me was to make me realise that one lives once – only once – and every moment is precious. Most of all, how families and friends are all important. I was so devastated on losing Francesca and can still feel the pain today. When I lost her that awful night, she took a little bit of me with her. The tears are never far away, and I have my own personal moment for her every day. I have a photograph of her in an oval frame, if it slips – which it does nearly every day, I straighten it. It is my way of letting her know she is a part of me never to be forgotten". As I write, I have a little photo of her by my computer".*
Islay would completely share those sentiments, although from a slightly different and less heart rending perspective, with the loss of her only sister at the age of 48 to cancer.

Islay's account: *"It is usually fairly predictable in life to lose one's parents, but to lose one's only sibling is harder to bear. When you lose your only sibling, a part of your childhood is lost forever, together with the ability to reminisce about things you uniquely shared, playing on family holidays, Christmases and such like. I miss her every day and have seized opportunities that maybe I would have been more cautious about, because she died before she was able to make those choices. I adore my only nephew – Robin, Dibby's son, whose eldest daughter Abigail is the image of my sister when she was a child and we were young girls growing up."*
"When you lose someone dear, there are lots of platitudes such as 'time is a great healer'. My personal opinion is that each loss leaves an enormous hole, a hole that can never be filled by that individual loss, a hole that initially I constantly fell into in the first few weeks and months after the bereavement. Each time I fell into it, I crawled my way out of the blackness and sadness, and carried on. After a while (time is indeterminate could be weeks, months or longer), I stopped falling into the hole and managed to walk around it but could still not look into the depths of its blackness which reflected the pain of my loss. Now I can walk around it, look into it and see the friendship, memories, sunshine, flowers, clouds and occasional thunder-storms that epitomised my loved one(s). Rarely do I fall in that hole now, but it is always there and is now managed

within my life, which has moved into another chapter without those special people. They are always in my heart and while I live that will never change".

Pammy and Islay share that same emotion of the awareness of life's fragility and the need to maximise every opportunity, as we never know what the future will hold. In memory of those we have loved and lost, we owe it to them to maximise the opportunities that our life gives us.

We write this through the Covid 19 pandemic of 2020, an experience unprecedented in any of our lifetimes. Captain Tom Moore, at the age of 99, set out to raise £1,000 by walking around his garden (using a Zimmer frame) 100 times before his 100th birthday, at the end of April. As we write this, the amount that has been donated is reaching over £30 million and still rising. This unequivocally demonstrates the amazing dedication and determination of the human spirit.

We hope that by the time this book is published Covid 19/Coronavirus will be a distant memory, although one of nightmare provoking proportions and generation changing ways we live life.

Riding schools MUST survive, in many cases they provide the ignition of a child's life-long commitment to the horse.

There are many riders from all disciplines whose first experience of horses was 'in a riding school'. This lights the hearts and minds of many a child and indeed if they have the talent and commitment, many a riding school has assisted in their chosen career pathway. Be it grooms to international horses, teachers either privately or in riding schools, or riders following their competitive career.

Talland School of Equitation has had through its doors: Anneli Drummond Hay (X ref. Ch 3), Captain Mark Phillips, Lucinda Green, John Francome, Ian Woodhead (X.Ref EFF ch 8) Adam

Kemp, Emile Faurie, (X.Ref EFF) and the list goes on. All received student training. In a way, the riding school sponsors the student's future career, the pay back being the work the individual does for that school.

Riding schools provide an inspiration to the adult that has always wanted to ride, but never had the opportunity, until now.

- You do not have to aspire to be an international rider, you can be a beginner, someone who has always wanted to ride.
- You can start in childhood or adulthood, and continue for life.
- Many Riding Schools run RDA (Riding for the Disabled session(s). The reason for it being such a successful sport for able and disabled, is the value to health both physically and mentally.
- Riding Schools provide a service from beginner to advanced, able bodied and disabled in the care, management and time required to involve horses in one's life.
- Riding Schools provide a safe, professional, fun environment to enthuse and facilitate horses into life, where the options of having a horse at home are not available.
- Many Riding Schools now have 'club' facilities where riders can share coffee, cakes and light meals in a social environment, before or after riding, where their passion can be shared and discussed with friends and other horse lovers.

In the next few paragraphs we provide case studies of two riding schools from both ends of the spectrum, giving the background to how they survived the dreaded Covid 19. The future is unclear, and the road to recovery will be tough but Riding Schools must survive as they are the life blood to many who aspire to ride and have no other avenue into 'horses for life'.

World famous Talland School of Equitation
Pammy and Brian Hutton head the family business that is 'Talland'. Students from all over the world come to train here at the school started by Pammy's Mother, the late Mrs Molly Sivewright FBHS, six decades ago, which is renowned as one of only a handful of establishments that continue to train riders from novice to international level.

Pammy documents here the way the Covid 19 pandemic is currently affecting 'Talland':

"During this Covid 19, that has taken lives of friends, staying cheerful, fighting to smile and selling oneself to a bank manager, has been a challenging time. Talland was one of the first three businesses in Gloucestershire to submit a 12 month business plan with a huge loss."

"At the time of writing we have no idea for the long-term survival, but nobody dies of hard work! I always enjoy the figures, but not this year, as the total loss for the year is likely to be approximately £200k. Every aspect of the business has been under scrutiny and interestingly enough I feel that some of the students, who are currently here in the lockdown, are some of the best that Talland has had in its 60 year history. I have tried to follow the Government guidelines but there has been some confusion and lack of common sense. We are all anxious to move to the 'new normal' perhaps returning to good old common sense borne on the practicality of dealing with horses, remembering the welfare of the horse (and rider)always comes first. As a professional I ride daily as part of my full time occupation. To be officially advised not to ride, while of course supporting the pressure on the NHS (if we fell off) was questionable advice to professional riders and the maintenance of working horses.

"Never have I been as upbeat or certain, knowing the future is possible due to my upbringing. Nothing is impossible, we can all help so much just by being positive. The only thing I haven't figured out is how to avoid death!"

Kate Pritchard runs Debdale Riding School near Kidderminster, Worcs. Islay has taught Kate, and her daughter Megan (now 22 and co proprietor of the school), for around 18 years of the 30 years the school has been in business.

Kate described the severe implications the lockdown has had on their business, which would cater extensively to local clientele, the beginner or inexperienced rider, children and some long term livery owners.

"The financial impact has been frightening, if not catastrophic. I know it may seem dramatic but Megan and I run the school on a very much 'hand to mouth' basis for both us and the horses. With no income, the fear of not being able to maintain the horses' welfare has proven to be very stressful. Our staff are self-employed, so we have not had to furlough them, but obviously without staff, the work load has fallen on Megan and myself to cover and we have 14 horses on site, 9 of whom live out. We have continued to offer all services required for the horses at livery. Owners have been allowed on the premises with all the guidelines in place for social distancing, hand washing, etc. and agreed time slots for visiting. As lockdown eased, we followed guidelines, introducing semi-private or private lessons to try and reinstate some income. In the long term there will be financial effects on the business. We have lost around £8,500 income from the school in 6 weeks. Thankfully we were eligible for a grant for rate relief and have been touched by the generosity of kind donations from clients. Without their help we would face an uncertain future. The horses' welfare, as I'm sure all schools large or small will emphasise, is paramount. Our school is our way of life, we will never be rich in cash but the joy, hard times, laughter and tears which our four-legged friends bring us, make it all worthwhile."

July 2020. Pammy's account:

We are taking small steps towards 'the new normal', an unmade road with very few signposts! Many are dragging along doggedly all the good stuff that came out of lockdown; determined to keep the better quality of life, the family time, the clean and tidy facilities. There is hope that we will all eventually recover financially and be brave enough to look at our bank accounts! Like so many other things in life today, we learn the state of our finances on-line and still feel the elation or despair as we look at the figures.

*What a pity then that we don't get that same 'feel' when we access learning on-line when it comes to Equestrianism! I have climbed all over my computer trying to 'feel' the softness or resistance whilst using my eyes and knowledge! I just love the **feel** of the horse that trusts me, who follows me in trot, who reins back from the word and allows me to share his energy. In the brave new world of computer learning 'feel' might fade away!*

With many colleges moving to 'e' learning, I wonder if this will start to cause a U turn in the trend of the last two decades for wannabe equestrians to start their journey in a college rather than in a working practical environment. 'e' learning like many equine college courses can so easily create the illusion that 'work' is a thing of the past. Keeping a yard of horses, be it a riding school or a competition yard involves hard work. Experience makes the work easier, both through repetition and physical development, just like horses. Those that gain 'experience' by attending a working yard for a few weeks, one day a week or from 'You Tube' will never develop the awareness, confidence, dexterity and coordination that working in our industry requires.

How therefore does one become the next Jennie Loriston Clarke MBE FBHS (see Ch 3), Judy Harvey FBHS (British Dressage director of International Teams and GB's chief selector.) certainly not at a computer terminal or in a class room! In a recent Education issue of Horse and Hound we saw one advertisement for a working yard offering training, swamped by adverts for college courses – are we all giving up? – will we all end up only offering 'e' learning! Much cheaper to go on line – one machine – no expense!

At Talland we are now back in business and can reintroduce the next generation to real riding, real life training and horses in real life.

After the 'full lockdown' I was amongst the first out on a horse riding a Grand Prix test with Dane Rawlings stunning idea at Hickstead (ref. Hickstead/ Rotterdam challenge) It felt like competing.

We are taught to think only positive thoughts and to reach high. I dreamt of the 90% and woke up and faced reality, no I prefer to think low, then everything else is an achievement! So centre line, wobble, flop, lacking impulsion and missed my changes! That's what I was worried about, but actually I rode a 'clear round'. Back home I did not feel low, worried or drink myself to sleep. I took the positive to work harder and it has helped my empathy teaching. Competing again reminds me of the terror and fear of 'not being good enough'. I just love competing and hear that it is the judges we have to beg to get brave. Ringing in my ears as I entered at 'A' was Dane Rawlings threat of refusal to administer CPR!

Not a day goes by where we do not learn something – Pammy is known to say: "when I'm 99 I will know everything – but be too old to impart it!"

Islay's account:

In coming to the conclusion of developing and producing this book with Pammy, we hope it will be published by Christmas 2020. This will see the end of a particularly traumatic year for us all. It has been completed during the most challenging and unexpected circumstances that anyone could have imagined or predicted, this time last year. We hope it will have some longevity – as do 'horses for life' in reality. Publishers have often said to me in the past when writing "avoid identifying time, as this will instantly 'date' the book and make it 'out of date in a year or two." I hope and believe that this ghastly pandemic will be managed (but probably not any time soon). It may be years, certainly many months or until the development of a reliable vaccine. We are old enough to remember Polio and Diphtheria being endemic. We will have to adapt to survive, sadly some will not be able to and will inevitably suffer financially, emotionally, physically, practically and some finally. We are as humans, adaptable and resilient, resourceful and hardworking, sharing, caring and supportive of each other, especially with those with whom we have developed a close bond. My personal learning through lockdown and since has been to accept *the things we cannot control (XRef the serenity prayer.Ch6), enjoy the moment as we never know when it will be snatched away from us. Spend time to value what we have around us, environment, home, family, friends, horses, dogs and for you 'whatever 'floats your boat'. 'Do as you would be done by', 'treat people the way you yourself would wish to be treated' and "Be nice to people on your way up because you'll meet them on your way down". So many 'off the tongue sayings' but profound meanings by which I personally try to live my life. In all cases I can attribute the 'love of the horse' as being a contributor to my mindset and learning from life. This book has been a joy to put together, but has also had moments where we have wanted to 'put it to bed'. As we said at the beginning, if it provides some interesting reading to a range of horse lovers and it helps any one of you reacquaint with a horse for the improvement of your soul, then it has served a purpose. In longevity may someone be reading this in years to come and remember 2020, the year Covid 19 impacted on our entire way of life and changed things for ever. Whether that change is for better or worse is completely up to every single one of us. Good luck for the future whatever that may hold. I finish my account of '**Horses for Life**' recalling a fridge magnet of which I am particularly fond. "I cannot imagine a heaven without horses in it."*

Leaving unanswered questions

- Where will the horse industry be into the next millennium?
- Will this book become an epic (we have mentioned 'Black Beauty' in this context) Oh joy if 'Horses for Life' became such a classic! - Dream on!
- Will the pervasive faction of society who feel that no one should be able to ride horses, run in races, make them jump fences or do fancy 'dressage tricks', have grown to have influence on the wonderful partnerships we share with horses today in so many ways, and discussed in this book?
- Will a pandemic like 'Covid 19' finally wipe us out globally, and then this planet can recover from the ravages that we humans have imposed on it?
- More simply will the human race of the 22nd century still enjoy this amazing relationship with 'the horse' that has given millions of us such enduring pleasure throughout our lives and for centuries before?

Reflections:

- Age certainly makes us more reflective, focusing on the good things in life, the privileges that have been conveyed on those of us that can and still do share our lives with horses.
- Giving due consideration to what has been learnt in previous generations and where necessary 'not throwing the baby out with the bath water' in the efforts to 'do it better in a more modern way'.

- The wish that we (all of us) will leave a legacy of knowledge and experience, which will continue to benefit the horse, through our successors.
- The urgency that the receding years convey on us, to maximise the time we have on this amazing planet, to benefit from all the wonders that it holds.
- To forgive us, if at times we have been 'nostalgic' for past joys of 'our generation', but then the initial idea behind this book was to celebrate the longevity that horses have with us in equestrian sport.
- The horse will always need care from a human being who identifies with him as a flight animal, a herd animal and a 'follower'. He will always need empathy and feel from those who share him for their own recreation and sport.
- To remember that the horse is a horse the world over and will continue to be so. Our wish is that those that come after us enjoy him and treat him with the reverence and respect that he so richly deserves.

Summary:

If you are reading this, then thank you for staying with us to the end. You may be reading the last page first, as some people do! If so, then please start at the beginning, and in either case, we hope you have found some inspiration from this book.

For all equestrians, the 'Horse of the Year Show' means a great deal, irrespective of which 'discipline' you favour. Founded in 1949 it is still regarded as the 'Finale of the Year'. The brainchild of Captain Tony Collins, and brought to life by the then Chairman of The British Show Jumping

Association (now British Showjumping – BS) – Colonel Sir Mike Ansell. The aim was a show that celebrated the Champion of Champions in many aspects of horsemanship. It has become the 'home' of many iconic competitions. The Leading Show Jumper of the Year, and the Pony Club Mounted Games final for the coveted 'Prince Philip Cup' to name just two. Revered by most ardent equestrians, it is five days of pure indulgence of 'the horse'. Due to its high standards of competition, qualification to ride there is hard fought, and a prized and valued goal in itself. The show is now widely regarded as the most famous Horse Show in the World.

Pammy won the Spillers Championship (Dressage with Show Jumping Competition) three times and her reflection on riding there was: "It always meant the world to me to ride at HOYS, and to win was incredibly special."

Islay's experience has been as a spectator, year on year, for decades. She reminisces: "As a pony club games fanatic, the closest I got to HOYS was for our team to be second in the regional final, when only the winning team went through to HOYS. We were devastated to get so close. Then the year I qualified a horse for the Spillers Championship, was the year I sold the horse for a price I could not refuse, and so I lost the ride. Again so near but yet so far!".

When we set out to write this book, it was primarily to celebrate the longevity of the horse as a lifelong partner or passion. It was also to consider the longevity of some of our top sporting icons within equestrian sport. As we developed the content, we expanded its remit to explore the intrinsic link of horse and human, its origins and future.

Between us, we have a shared life's experience of some combined 140 years with horses and we never stop learning. In fact we both feel that we knew a little at the beginning of our 'life with horses', then we learnt a bit more, and now we know a little more still, but we also know how much more there is waiting to be learnt. It is the horses that teach us, and it is the learning that is so motivating and inspirational. We have both had decades of practise of learning, so why would we stop now when we are quite good at it? Now it comes easily and we thrive on it. Continually learning keeps us current, it keeps us 'moving forward', it helps us 'keep up' and it can only be in the best interests of the horse, and that is the prime 'raison d'etre'. If we don't know something, "we find someone who does!", we get the answer and therefore we continually learn. It has been a true labour of love to bring this book to fruition.

The finale at the Horse of the year Show is one of the most moving experiences you will ever experience if you love horses. The arena is full of all the winning horses, the heavy horses, the pony club mounted games teams, the celebrity performers and the show jumpers. The arena falls silent and all the horses stand motionless, uncannily aware of the importance and solemnity of the moment. The 'ode to the horse' brings this world-famous show to a timeless conclusion.

There can be no better way to end this book than to use this amazing poem that was written by Robert Duncan, a friend of Sir Mike Ansell (founder of Horse of the year Show - HOYS). We contacted Robert's Granddaughter, in our quest to use this wonderfully moving and appropriate finale for our book. She graciously gave us permission, whilst obviously we agreed to attribute it to the author Robert Duncan.

"ODE TO THE HORSE"
By Robert Duncan

Where in this wide world can men find nobility without pride,
Friendship without envy, or beauty without vanity?
Here, where grace is laced with power and strength by gentleness confined.
He serves without servility, he has fought without enmity.
There is nothing so powerful, nothing less violent.
There is nothing so quick, nothing more patient.
Our pioneers were borne on his back.
Our history is his industry.
We are his heirs and he is our inheritance.
THE HORSE!

BV - #0052 - 141220 - C0 - 229/152/11 - PB - 9781913425531